Hands-On One-shot Learning with Python

Learn to implement fast and accurate deep learning models with fewer training samples using PyTorch

Shruti Jadon
Ankush Garg

BIRMINGHAM - MUMBAI

Hands-On One-shot Learning with Python

Commissioning Editor: Amey Varangaonkar
Acquisition Editor: Yogesh Deokar
Content Development Editor: Athikho Sapuni Rishana
Senior Editor: Sofi Rogers
Technical Editor: Manikandan Kurup
Copy Editor: Safis Editing
Project Coordinator: Aishwarya Mohan
Proofreader: Safis Editing
Indexer: Priyanka Dhadke
Production Designer: Jyoti Chauhan

First published: April 2020

Production reference: 1090420

Published by Packt Publishing Ltd.
Livery Place
35 Livery Street
Birmingham
B3 2PB, UK.

ISBN 978-1-83882-546-1

www.packtpub.com

Packt.com

Subscribe to our online digital library for full access to over 7,000 books and videos, as well as industry leading tools to help you plan your personal development and advance your career. For more information, please visit our website.

Why subscribe?

- Spend less time learning and more time coding with practical eBooks and Videos from over 4,000 industry professionals

- Improve your learning with Skill Plans built especially for you

- Get a free eBook or video every month

- Fully searchable for easy access to vital information

- Copy and paste, print, and bookmark content

Did you know that Packt offers eBook versions of every book published, with PDF and ePub files available? You can upgrade to the eBook version at www.packt.com and as a print book customer, you are entitled to a discount on the eBook copy. Get in touch with us at customercare@packtpub.com for more details.

At www.packt.com, you can also read a collection of free technical articles, sign up for a range of free newsletters, and receive exclusive discounts and offers on Packt books and eBooks.

About the authors

Shruti Jadon is currently working as a Machine Learning Software Engineer at Juniper Networks, Sunnyvale and visiting Researcher at Rhode Island Hospital (Brown University). She has obtained her master's degree in Computer Science from University of Massachusetts, Amherst. Her research interests include deep learning architectures, computer vision, and convex optimization. In the past, she has worked at Autodesk, Quantiphi, SAP Labs, and Snapdeal.

Ankush Garg is currently working as a Software Engineer in the auto-translation team at Google, Mountain View. He has obtained his master's degree in Computer Science from the University of Massachusetts, Amherst, and his bachelor's at NSIT, Delhi. His research interests include language modeling, model compression, and optimization. In the past, he has worked as a Software Engineer at Amazon, India.

About the reviewer

Greg Walters has been involved with computers and computer programming since 1972. He is well versed in Visual Basic, Visual Basic.NET, Python, and SQL, and is an accomplished user of MySQL, SQLite, Microsoft SQL Server, Oracle, C++, Delphi, Modula-2, Pascal, C, 80x86 Assembler, COBOL, and Fortran. He is a programming trainer and has trained numerous individuals in many pieces of computer software, including MySQL, Open Database Connectivity, Quattro Pro, Corel Draw!, Paradox, Microsoft Word, Excel, DOS, Windows 3.11, Windows for Workgroups, Windows 95, Windows NT, Windows 2000, Windows XP, and Linux. He is currently retired and, in his spare time, is a musician and loves to cook. He is also open to working as a freelancer on various projects.

Packt is searching for authors like you

If you're interested in becoming an author for Packt, please visit `authors.packtpub.com` and apply today. We have worked with thousands of developers and tech professionals, just like you, to help them share their insight with the global tech community. You can make a general application, apply for a specific hot topic that we are recruiting an author for, or submit your own idea.

Table of Contents

Preface

One-shot learning has been an active field of research for many scientists who are trying to find a cognitive machine that is as close to human beings as possible in terms of learning. As there are various theories as to how humans effect one-shot learning, there are a variety of different methods available to achieve this, ranging from non-parametric models and deep learning architectures to probabilistic models.

Hands-On One-shot Learning with Python will focus on designing and learning about models that can learn information relating to an object from one, or only a few, training examples. The book will begin by giving you a brief overview of deep learning and one-shot learning to get you started. Then, you will learn different methods to achieve this, including non-parametric models, deep learning architectures, and probabilistic models. Once you are well versed in the core principles, you will explore some of the practical real-world examples and implementations of one-shot learning using scikit-learn and PyTorch.

By the end of the book, you will be familiar with one-shot and few-shots learning methods and be able to accelerate your deep learning processes with one-shot learning.

Who this book is for

AI researchers, as well as machine learning and deep learning experts who wish to apply one-shot learning to reduce the overall training time of their models, will find this book to be a very good introductory source of learning.

What this book covers

Chapter 1, *Introduction to One-shot Learning*, tells us what one-shot learning is and how it works. It also tells us about the human brain's workings and how it translates to machine learning.

Chapter 2, *Metrics-Based Methods*, explores methods that use different forms of embeddings, and evaluation metrics, by keeping the core as basic k-nearest neighbors.

Chapter 3, *Model-Based Methods*, explores two architectures whose internal architectures help to train a k-shot learning model.

Chapter 4, *Optimization-Based Methods*, explores different forms of optimization algorithms, which help in improving accuracy even when the volume of data is low.

Chapter 5, *Generative Modeling-Based Methods*, explores the development of a Bayesian learning framework based on representing object categories with probabilistic models.

Chapter 6, *Conclusions and Other Approaches*, goes through certain aspects of architecture, metrics, and algorithms to understand how we can determine whether an approach is close to human brain capability.

To get the most out of this book

Knowledge of basic machine learning and deep learning concepts and the underlying math, as well as some exposure to Python programming, will be required for this book.

Software/Hardware covered in this book	OS requirements
Software: Jupyter Notebook, Anaconda Language and Libraries: Python 3.X and above, PyTorch 1.4, Scikit-learn.	Any OS (Linux environment is preferable).
Hardware: None. But if you wish to increase the speed of training. You can use the same codes with minor modifications on GPU Hardware.	

If you are using the digital version of this book, we advise you to type the code yourself or access the code via the GitHub repository (link available in the next section). Doing so will help you avoid any potential errors related to the copying and pasting of code.

Download the example code files

You can download the example code files for this book from your account at www.packt.com. If you purchased this book elsewhere, you can visit www.packt.com/support and register to have the files emailed directly to you.

You can download the code files by following these steps:

1. Log in or register at www.packt.com.
2. Select the **SUPPORT** tab.
3. Click on **Code Downloads & Errata**.
4. Enter the name of the book in the **Search** box and follow the onscreen instructions.

Once the file is downloaded, please make sure that you unzip or extract the folder using the latest version of:

- WinRAR/7-Zip for Windows
- Zipeg/iZip/UnRarX for Mac
- 7-Zip/PeaZip for Linux

The code bundle for the book is also hosted on GitHub at `https://github.com/PacktPublishing/Hands-On-One-shot-Learning-with-Python`. In case there's an update to the code, it will be updated on the existing GitHub repository.

We also have other code bundles from our rich catalog of books and videos available at `https://github.com/PacktPublishing/`. Check them out!

Download the color images

We also provide a PDF file that has color images of the screenshots/diagrams used in this book. You can download it here: `http://www.packtpub.com/sites/default/files/downloads/9781838825461_ColorImages.pdf`.

Conventions used

There are a number of text conventions used throughout this book.

`CodeInText`: Indicates code words in text, database table names, folder names, filenames, file extensions, pathnames, dummy URLs, user input, and Twitter handles. Here is an example: "Import the `iris` dataset."

A block of code is set as follows:

```
# import small dataset
iris = datasets.load_iris()
X = iris.data
y = iris.target
```

When we wish to draw your attention to a particular part of a code block, the relevant lines or items are set in bold:

```
[2 1 2 1 2 0 1 0 0 0 2 1 1 0 0 0 2 2 1 2 1 0 0 1 2 0 0 2 0 0]
```

Any command-line input or output is written as follows:

```
pip install -r requirements.txt
```

Bold: Indicates a new term, an important word, or words that you see onscreen. For example, words in menus or dialog boxes appear in the text like this. Here is an example: "We can use a new loss function known as **triplet loss**, which helps the architecture to get better results."

Warnings or important notes appear like this.

Tips and tricks appear like this.

Get in touch

Feedback from our readers is always welcome.

General feedback: If you have questions about any aspect of this book, mention the book title in the subject of your message and email us at customercare@packtpub.com.

Errata: Although we have taken every care to ensure the accuracy of our content, mistakes do happen. If you have found a mistake in this book, we would be grateful if you would report this to us. Please visit www.packt.com/submit-errata, selecting your book, clicking on the Errata Submission Form link, and entering the details.

Piracy: If you come across any illegal copies of our works in any form on the internet, we would be grateful if you would provide us with the location address or website name. Please contact us at copyright@packt.com with a link to the material.

If you are interested in becoming an author: If there is a topic that you have expertise in, and you are interested in either writing or contributing to a book, please visit authors.packtpub.com.

Reviews

Please leave a review. Once you have read and used this book, why not leave a review on the site that you purchased it from? Potential readers can then see and use your unbiased opinion to make purchase decisions, we at Packt can understand what you think about our products, and our authors can see your feedback on their book. Thank you!

For more information about Packt, please visit `packt.com`.

Section 1: One-shot Learning Introduction

Deep learning has brought about a major change to industry—be it manufacturing, medical, or human resources. With this major revolution and proof of concept, almost every industry is trying to adapt its business model to comply with deep learning, but it has some major requirements that may not fit every business or industry. After reading this section, you will have a proper understanding of the pros and cons of deep learning.

This section comprises the following chapter:

- Chapter 1, *Introduction to One-shot Learning*

1
Introduction to One-shot Learning

Humans can learn new things with a small set of examples. When presented with stimuli, humans seem to be able to understand new concepts quickly and then recognize variations of those concepts in the future. A child can learn to recognize a dog from a single picture, but a machine learning system needs a lot of examples to learn the features of a dog and recognize them in the future. Machine learning, as a field, has been highly successful at a variety of tasks, such as classification and web searching, as well as image and speech recognition. Often, however, these models do not perform well without a large amount of data (examples) to learn from. The primary motivation behind this book is to train a model with very few examples that is capable of generalizing to unfamiliar categories without extensive retraining.

Deep learning has played an important role in the advancement of machine learning, but it also requires large datasets. Different techniques, such as regularization, can reduce overfitting in low-data regimes, but do not solve the inherent problem that comes with fewer training examples. Furthermore, the large size of datasets leads to slow learning, requiring many weight updates using gradient descent. This is mostly due to the parametric aspect of an ML algorithm, in which training examples need to be slowly learned. In contrast, many known non-parametric models such as nearest neighbor do not require any training, but performance depends on a sometimes arbitrarily chosen distance metric such as the L2 distance. One-shot learning is an object categorization problem in computer vision. While most ML-based object categorization algorithms require hundreds or thousands of images and very large datasets to train on, one-shot learning aims to learn information about object categories from one, or only a few, training images. In this chapter, we will learn about the basics of one-shot learning and explore its real-world applications.

The following topics will be covered in this chapter:

- The human brain—overview
- Machine learning—history overview
- One-shot learning—overview
- Setting up your environment
- Coding exercise

Technical requirements

The following libraries will be required to learn and execute the project in this chapter:

- Python
- Anaconda
- Jupyter Notebook
- PyTorch
- Matplotlib
- Scikit-learn

You can find the code files for this chapter in the GitHub repository of this book: `https://github.com/PacktPublishing/Hands-on-One-Shot-Learning-with-Python`.

The human brain – overview

The human brain has been a subject of research since the beginning of civilization. If we look into the development of a child, we will observe that as they grow, their ability to learn also grows. First, they learn about food, then they learn to identify faces. Every time a child learns something, information is encoded into some portion of the brain. Still, the real question remains, how does information get stored in our brains? Why is some information hardcoded, yet other information is easily forgotten?

How the human brain learns

Most of the information on how the brain trains itself to process data is unknown, but there are various theories that explore it. If we look into the structure of a brain's neuron, as shown in the following diagram, a neuron works similar to a collector, wherein it collects signals from other neurons through **dendrites**. Once the signal becomes strong, the neuron sends out an electrical signal through thin strands known as **axons** to nearby neurons. At the end of this network, the synapse converts the signal activity into an excitation activity and activates the connected neurons. Brain neurons learn to send signals to different parts of the brain by changing the effectiveness of the synapse, similar to how some weights become close to zero for certain neurons in an artificial neural network:

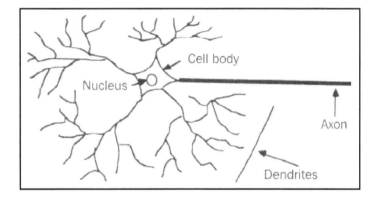

There are a lot of theories to suggest that dense connections among neurons increase the ability of humans to learn. In turn, many neuroscientists believe that dense dendrite connectivity is created as the brain is used more through learning and stimulation. Hence, we become more intelligent as we learn more and more.

Comparing human neurons and artificial neurons

Though the human neuron has been the inspiration for creating artificial neural networks, there are several ways in which they are dissimilar. Researchers are trying to bridge these gaps by experimenting with different activation (excitation) functions and non-linear systems. Similar to how our brain has a collection of neurons that transmit and process the information received from our senses, a neural network also consists of layers (a group of neurons) that learns about tasks by transmitting information across layers. In certain cases, we can say an artificial neuron works in a similar way to a neuron present in our brain. Let's look at the following diagram:

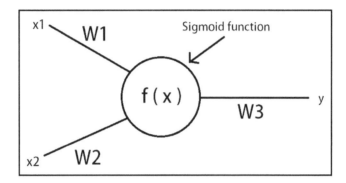

As we can see in the preceding diagram, information flows through each connection, and each connection has a specific weight, which controls the flow of data. If we compare a human brain neuron's activity with artificial neural networks, we will see that whenever we create a neural network for a task, it is like creating a new brain neuron. If we look around us, we have already started relying on computers to make decisions, for example, in the case of credit card fraud, spam/non-spam emails, and recommendation systems. It's like we have created new brains for small tasks around us. Still, the question remains, what is the difference between human and artificial neural networks? Let's find out:

- One of the major differences is the amount of learning data required. For a neural network to learn, we need a lot of data, whereas a human brain can learn with less data. If we wish to have a neural network with a similar capacity to a human brain, we need to improve upon existing optimization algorithms.
- Another key difference is speed. Often, neural networks process data and information much more quickly than humans.

Machine learning – historical overview

Machine learning is a program that, given a task (loss function), learns through experience (training data). With experience, that program learns to perform the given task to a desirable standard. During the 1960s, machine learning was majorly focused on creating different forms of data preprocessing filters. With the introduction of image filters, the focus then shifted toward computer vision, and major research work was undertaken in this domain during the 1990s and 2000s. After some stability in terms of traditional machine learning algorithms being developed, researchers moved to the probabilistic domain, as it became more promising with the introduction of high-dimensional data. Deep learning bloomed when it won the ImageNet Challenge in 2012, and has since taken on an important role in the field of data science.

Machine learning can be classified into two categories:

- **Parametric**: Learning is accomplished by using an algorithm to adapt the parameters in a mathematical or statistical model given training data, such as logistic regression, support vector machines, and neural networks.
- **Nonparametric**: Learning is accomplished by storing the training data (memorization) and performing some dimensionality reduction mappings, for example, **k-nearest neighbor** (**kNN**) and decision trees.

Due to the requirement of learning parameters, the parametric approach usually requires a large amount of data. Incidentally, if we have a large number of datasets, it's best to use a parametric approach, as a nonparametric approach generally requires storing data and processing it for every query.

Challenges in machine learning and deep learning

Machine learning and deep learning have revolutionized the computer science industry, but they have advantages and disadvantages. Some of the common challenges faced by our current approaches are as follows:

- **Data gathering**: Collecting sufficient relevant data for each category for machines to learn is laborious.
- **Data labeling**: Often, labeling data requires experts or is impossible due to privacy, safety, or ethical issues.

- **Hardware constraints**: Due to the large amount of data, as well as large parametric models, expensive hardware (GPUs and TPUs) is required to train them.
- **Result analysis**: Understanding the result is also a major challenge, though there are certain open source libraries that provide analysis parameters.

Apart from these challenges, machine learning also faces challenges in dealing with feature selection and higher-dimensional data.

In the next section, we will introduce one-shot learning and learn how it attempts to solve the challenges faced by machine learning and deep learning.

One-shot learning – overview

One-shot learning can be seen as an approach to train machines in a way that is similar to how humans learn. One-shot learning is an approach to learn a new task using limited supervised data with the help of strong prior knowledge. The first work published that resulted in high accuracy for the image classification problem dates back to the 2000s by Dr. Fei Fei Li—although, in recent years, researchers have made good progress tackling it through different deep learning architectures and optimization algorithms, such as matching networks, model agnostic meta-learning, and memory-augmented neural networks. One-shot learning has a lot of applications in several industries—the medical and manufacturing industries in particular. In medicine, we can use one-shot learning when there is limited data available, for example, when working with rare diseases; whereas in manufacturing, we can reduce man-made errors such as edge case manufacturing defects.

Prerequisites of one-shot learning

If we look into further discussion about how we can learn necessary information from a limited amount of data, we will realize that the human brain already has neurons trained to extract important information. For example, if a child has been taught that a spherical object is a ball, their brain also processes information about the ball's size and texture—also known as **filters** of the object. So, for any form of one-shot learning, we can say we need at least one of the following things:

- Previously trained filters and a pre-determined architecture
- A correct assumption of data distribution
- A definite form of taxonomy for information stored or collected

In certain cases, we observe that we can only have a very low level of feature extraction. In those scenarios, we can just rely on a nonparametric or probabilistic approach because, to learn parameters, we need a sufficient amount of data. Even if we somehow force a neural network to learn with hardly any data, it will result in overfitting.

In the next section, we will do a short coding exercise to see how, when we have a small dataset, a simple nonparametric kNN performs better than neural networks. Unfortunately, it probably wouldn't work very well in the real world, as we still have the problems of learning a good feature representation and choosing an appropriate distance function.

Types of one-shot learning

There are various approaches to solve one-shot learning. Roughly speaking, they can be organized into five main categories:

- Data augmentation methods
- Model-based methods
- Metrics-based methods
- Optimization-based methods
- Generative modeling-based methods

The following diagram shows the categories of one-shot learning:

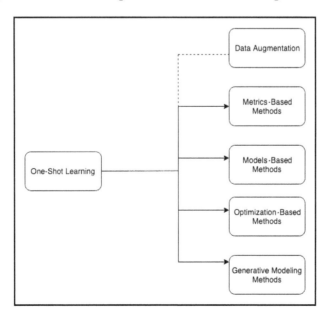

Data augmentation is the most commonly used method in the deep learning community to add variations to data, increase data size, and balance data. It's achieved by adding some form of noise in the data. For instance, images might be scaled, translated, and rotated; whereas in a natural language processing task, there might be synonym replacement, random insertions, and random swaps.

Though data augmentation methods play a crucial role in preprocessing, we won't be covering that topic in this book. In this book, we will focus on algorithmic approaches of one-shot learning and how to implement them. We will also experiment with them on commonly used one-shot learning datasets such as the **Omniglot** dataset and **Mini ImageNet**.

Setting up your environment

In this section, we will set up a virtual environment for our coding exercise and questions using the following steps:

1. Clone the repository by going into the directory of your choice and running the following command in the Git Bash command line:

   ```
   git clone
   https://github.com/Packt-Publishing/Hands-on-One-Shot-Learning.git
   ```

2. Go to the `Chapter01` directory of the cloned repository:

   ```
   cd Hands-on-One-Shot-Learning/Chapter01
   ```

3. Then, open a Terminal and use the following command to install Anaconda for Python, version 3.6 (`https://docs.anaconda.com/anaconda/install/`), and create a virtual environment:

   ```
   conda create --name environment_name python=3.6
   ```

    In *steps 3* and *4*, you can replace `environment_name` with an easy name to remember, such as `one_shot`, or a name of your choice.

4. Activate the environment using the following command:

   ```
   source activate environment_name
   ```

5. Install `requirements.txt` using the following command:

```
pip install -r requirements.txt
```

6. Run the following command to open Jupyter Notebook:

```
jupyter notebook
```

Now that we have set up the environment, let's go ahead with the coding exercise.

Coding exercise

In this section, we will explore a basic one-shot learning approach. As humans, we have a hierarchical way of thinking. For example, if we see something unknown to us, we look for its similarity to objects we already know. Similarly, in this exercise, we will use a nonparametric kNN approach to find classes. We will also compare its performance to the basic neural network architecture.

kNN – basic one-shot learning

In this exercise, we will compare kNN to neural networks where we have a small dataset. We will be using the `iris` dataset imported from the `scikit-learn` library.

To begin, we will first discuss the basics of kNN. The kNN classifier is a nonparametric classifier that simply stores the training data, *D*, and classifies each new instance using a majority vote over its set of *k* nearest neighbors, computed using any distance function. For a kNN, we need to choose the distance function, *d*, and the number of neighbors, *k*:

$$f_{knn}(x) = argmax \sum_{i \epsilon N(x)} I[y_i = y]$$

You can also refer to the code file at the following GitHub link:
https://github.com/PacktPublishing/Hands-on-One-Shot-Learning-wi
th-Python/blob/master/Chapter01/CodingExercise01.ipynb.

Follow these steps to compare kNN with a neural network:

1. Import all the libraries required for this exercise using the following code:

```
import numpy as np
import matplotlib.pyplot as plt
from sklearn import datasets
from sklearn.neighbors import KNeighborsClassifier
from sklearn.model_selection import train_test_split
from sklearn.metrics import confusion_matrix, accuracy_score
from sklearn.model_selection import cross_val_score
from sklearn.neural_network import MLPClassifier
```

2. Import the `iris` dataset:

```
# import small dataset
iris = datasets.load_iris()
X = iris.data
y = iris.target
```

3. To ensure we are using a very small dataset, we will randomly choose 30 points and print them using the following code:

```
indices=np.random.choice(len(X), 30)
X=X[indices]
y=y[indices]
print (y)
```

This will be the resultant output:

```
[2 1 2 1 2 0 1 0 0 0 2 1 1 0 0 0 2 2 1 2 1 0 0 1 2 0 0 2 0 0]
```

4. To understand our features, we will try to plot them in 3D as a scatterplot:

```
from mpl_toolkits.mplot3d import Axes3D
fig = plt.figure(1, figsize=(20, 15))
ax = Axes3D(fig, elev=48, azim=134)
ax.scatter(X[:, 0], X[:, 1], X[:, 2], c=y,
          cmap=plt.cm.Set1, edgecolor='k', s = X[:, 3]*50)

for name, label in [('Virginica', 0), ('Setosa', 1),
('Versicolour', 2)]:
   ax.text3D(X[y == label, 0].mean(),
             X[y == label, 1].mean(),
             X[y == label, 2].mean(), name,
             horizontalalignment='center',
             bbox=dict(alpha=.5, edgecolor='w',
facecolor='w'),size=25)
```

```
ax.set_title("3D visualization", fontsize=40)
ax.set_xlabel("Sepal Length [cm]", fontsize=25)
ax.w_xaxis.set_ticklabels([])
ax.set_ylabel("Sepal Width [cm]", fontsize=25)
ax.w_yaxis.set_ticklabels([])
ax.set_zlabel("Petal Length [cm]", fontsize=25)
ax.w_zaxis.set_ticklabels([])

plt.show()
```

The following plot is the output. As we can see in the 3D visualization, data points are usually found in groups:

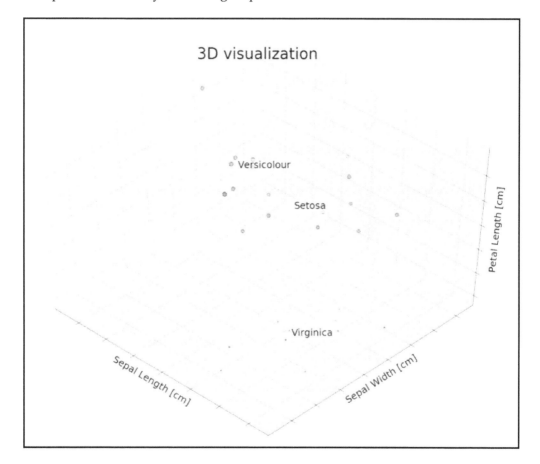

5. To begin with, we will first split the dataset into training and testing sets using an 80:20 split. We will be using `k=3` as the nearest neighbor:

```
X_train, X_test, y_train, y_test = train_test_split(X, y, test_size
= 0.2, random_state = 0)
# Instantiate learning model (k = 3)
classifier = KNeighborsClassifier(n_neighbors=3)

# Fitting the model
classifier.fit(X_train, y_train)

# Predicting the Test set results
y_pred = classifier.predict(X_test)

cm = confusion_matrix(y_test, y_pred)

accuracy = accuracy_score(y_test, y_pred)*100
print('Accuracy of our model is equal ' + str(round(accuracy, 2)) +
' %.')
```

This will result in the following output:

```
Accuracy of our model is equal 83.33 %.
```

6. Initialize the hidden layers' sizes and the number of iterations:

```
mlp = MLPClassifier(hidden_layer_sizes=(13,13,13),max_iter=10)
mlp.fit(X_train,y_train)
```

 You might get some warnings, depending on the version of scikit-learn, such as `/sklearn/neural_network/multilayer_perceptron.py:562:Conv ergenceWarning: Stochastic Optimizer: Maximum iterations (10) reached and the optimization hasn't converged yet. % self.max_iter, ConvergenceWarning)`. It's just an indication that your model isn't converged yet.

7. We will predict our test dataset for both kNN and a neural network and then compare the two:

```
predictions = mlp.predict(X_test)

accuracy = accuracy_score(y_test, predictions)*100
print('Accuracy of our model is equal ' + str(round(accuracy, 2)) +
' %.')
```

The following is the resultant output:

```
Accuracy of our model is equal 50.0 %.
```

For our current scenario, we can see that the neural network is less accurate than the kNN. This could be due to a lot of reasons, including the randomness of the dataset, the choice of neighbors, and the number of layers. But if we run it enough times, we will observe that a kNN is more likely to give a better output as it always stores data points, instead of learning parameters as neural networks do. Therefore, a kNN can be called a one-shot learning method.

Summary

Deep learning has revolutionized the field of data science and it is still making progress, but there are still major industries that are yet to experience all of the advantages of deep learning, such as the medical and manufacturing industries. The zenith of human achievement will be to create a machine that can learn as humans do and that can become an expert in the same way humans can. Successful deep learning, though, usually comes with the prerequisite of having very large datasets to work from. Fortunately, this book focuses on architectures that can do away with this prerequisite.

In this chapter, we learned about the human brain and how the structure of an artificial neural network is close to the structure of our brain. We introduced the basic concepts of machine learning and deep learning, along with their challenges. We also discussed one-shot learning and its various types, and later experimented with the `iris` dataset to compare a parametric and nonparametric approach in a scarce data situation. Overall, we concluded that proper feature representation plays an important role in determining the efficiency of a machine learning model.

In the next chapter, we will learn about metrics-based one-shot learning methods and explore the feature extraction domain of one-shot learning algorithms.

Questions

- Why does a kNN work better than a newly trained artificial neural network for a one-shot learning task?
- What are nonparametric machine learning algorithms?
- Are decision trees a parametric or nonparametric algorithm?
- Experiment with other classification algorithms as a coding exercise and compare the results.

Section 2: Deep Learning Architectures 2

One-shot learning has been an active field of research for many scientists who are trying to find a cognitive machine that is as close as possible to humans in terms of learning. As there are various theories about how humans do one-shot learning, we have a lot of different deep learning methods that we can use to solve it. This section of the book will focus on metrics-based, model-based, and optimization-based deep learning architectures to tackle one-shot learning problems, along with their implementations.

This section comprises the following chapters:

- Chapter 2, *Metrics-Based Methods*
- Chapter 3, *Model-Based Methods*
- Chapter 4, *Optimization-Based Methods*

Metrics-Based Methods

2

Deep learning has successfully achieved state-of-the-art performance in a variety of applications, such as image classification, object detection, speech recognition, and so on. But deep learning architectures often fail when forced to make predictions about data for which there is little supervised information available. As we know, mathematics is fundamental to all machine learning and deep learning models; we convey our data and objectives to machines using mathematical representations of the data. These representations can have many forms, especially if we want to learn complex tasks (for example, disease detection), or if we want our architecture to learn representations based on different objectives, for example, to calculate the similarity between two images, we can calculate both Euclidean distances and cosine similarity.

In this chapter, we will learn about deep learning architectures that can learn proper mathematical representations from smaller datasets. Overall, we aim to create an architecture that can generalize unfamiliar categories without extensive data collections or training processes.

The following topics will be covered in this chapter:

- Parametric methods – an overview
- Siamese networks
- Matching networks
- A coding exercise

Technical requirements

The following libraries will be required to learn and execute the project in this chapter:

- Python
- Anaconda
- Jupyter Notebook
- PyTorch
- Matplotlib
- scikit-learn

You can find the code file for the chapter in the GitHub repo of the book, at `https://github.com/PacktPublishing/Hands-On-One-shot-Learning-with-Python`.

Parametric methods – an overview

In the previous chapter, we briefly discussed non-parametric machine learning methods. This section will be primarily focused on what the parametric methods of machine learning are, and what they actually learn.

In simple terms, parametric machine learning algorithms try to learn the joint probabilistic distribution of data and their labels. The parameters we learn are of the equation given by joint probabilistic distribution; for example, as we know, logistic regression can be seen as a one-layered neural network. So, considering a one-layered neural network, what it actually learns is the weights and biases of the equation, so as to fit $P(Y/X)$ to the possible categorical distribution of Y*(labels)*.

Logistic regression is a form of **discriminative classifier**, and in discriminative classifiers, we only focus on $P(Y/X)$, that is, we make an assumption about the probabilistic distribution of *Labels(Y)*, and try to somehow map our *Input(X)* to it. So, essentially what we try to do in logistic regression is the following:

$$F_{LogisticRegression}(X, Y) = argmax_{c \in y} P(Y = c|X)$$

Here, $P(Y|X)$ is a categorical distribution, which means that we are trying to learn a distribution over possible categories. In simpler terms: given X, we will learn all the possible categories that Y can have. This is all possible due to the data—as the amount of data increases, our approximation of Y also increases. In the next section, we will go through the learning procedure of neural networks, and see what attributes play an important part in approximating Y labels.

Neural networks – learning procedure

As we know, neural networks learn through minimizing the loss function (or the objective function) using the stochastic gradient descent optimization method. So, loss functions are one of the major factors that determine the objective of neural network architecture. For example, if we want to classify data points, we will choose loss functions such as **categorical cross-entropy**, **0-1 loss**, and **hinge loss**; whereas, if our objective is regression, we will choose loss functions such as **mean squared error**, **root mean squared error**, and **Huber loss**. Some of the common equations are as follows:

$$\text{Cross-Entropy}\backslash\text{Loss} = \left(-y * log\big(f(x_i)\big) - (1-y) * log\big(1 - f(x_i)\big) \right)$$

$$\text{Squared error} = \big(y_i - f(x_i)\big)^2$$

$$\text{Absolute error} = |y_i - f(x_i)|$$

$$\text{Squared loss} = \big(1 - \tilde{y}_i f(x_i)\big)^2$$

$$\text{0-1 loss} = I\big(\tilde{y}_i \neq f(x_i)\big)$$

$$\text{Exponential loss} = exp\big(-\tilde{y}_i f(x_i)\big)$$

$$\text{Log loss} = \frac{1}{log\,2} log\big(1 + e^{-\tilde{y}_i f(x_i)}\big)$$

$$\text{Hinge loss} = |1 - \tilde{y}_i f(x_i)|_+$$

The first thing that comes to everyone's mind after knowing that loss functions have a major effect on neural networks is that we need to come up with better loss functions. If you look into the latest research, you'll see that major developments have been made on the basis of changing loss functions for object detection, image segmentation, machine translation, and so on. Figuring out a new loss function can be tricky due to two reasons:

- The objective function has to be convex in nature to meet the requirements of stochastic gradient descent optimization.
- Often, the minima obtained by different functions is the same numerically.

In the next section, we will go through understanding how these loss functions help an architecture learn different image features, and how we can incorporate these features to train a model for various other objectives.

Visualizing parameters

Neural networks learn through gradient descent, but what do they learn? The answer is parameters, but we are looking to understand what those parameters mean. In the following diagram, if we look at the first few layers, we will see simple and comprehensible extracted features, such as edges and interest points, whereas deeper layer features are more complex. For example, if we look at the last layer in the following diagram, we will observe that features are indecipherable compared to the initial layer features. This is because as we go into deeper layers, more information-rich features are being extracted through various matrix operations. This enables high-dimensional information to be compressed into the low-dimensional loss function space and results in a trained model:

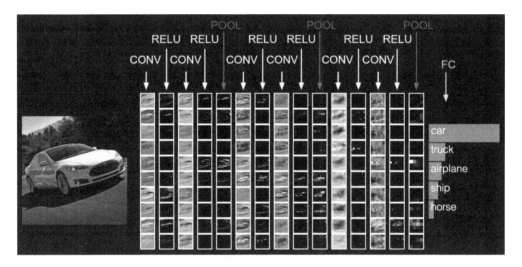

So, for example, if we are looking at categories such as flower versus car, the initial layers' features would be sufficient. But if we have categories such as types of cars, we need a deeper model, as we need to extract more complicated features, which requires a larger dataset. The question is, what decides the kind of features or parameters that a model learns, and is it possible to learn these important parameters at initial layers? In the next section, we will explore Siamese networks, a neural network architecture that can learn complex features in the first few layers by changing the loss function and its architectural design.

Understanding Siamese networks

A Siamese network, as the name suggests, is an architecture with two parallel layers. In this architecture, instead of a model learning to classify its inputs using classification loss functions, the model learns to differentiate between two given inputs. It compares two inputs based on a similarity metric and checks whether they are the same. Similar to any deep learning architecture, a Siamese network also has two phases—a training and a testing phase. But, for a one-shot learning approach (as we won't have a lot of data points), we will be training the model architecture on one dataset and testing it on a different dataset. To put this in simpler terms, we learn image embeddings using a supervised metric-based approach with Siamese neural networks, and then reuse that network's features for one-shot learning without fine-tuning or retraining.

Extraction of good features for machine learning algorithms plays a crucial role in determining the efficiency of a model. In various scenarios, it is proven to be either computationally expensive or difficult when we have limited data available.

As we can see in the following diagram, our objective is to train a network to understand whether two images or sounds are the same. Say that in the first image, we have two footballs; even if the background is different, both are footballs, so it is considered the same. The case is similar for the sound of the word "cow". Where images and sounds are different, as in the case of a crocodile and a football, they are labeled as **different**:

	same	"cow" (speaker #1)	"cow" (speaker #2)	same	
	different	"cow" (speaker #1)	"cat" (speaker #2)	different	
	same	"can" (speaker #1)	"can" (speaker #2)	same	
	different	"can" (speaker #1)	"cab" (speaker #2)	different	

The key idea might sound similar to transfer learning, but it is a little different. Siamese networks learn these features using the contrastive loss function. Secondly, a Siamese network approach is only valid for similar domains, as it also needs to take care of domain adaption, that is, it needs to try to ensure that our training and testing datasets are close in terms of the domain. For example, if you want to create a system to test whether two handwriting examples belong to the same person, you can train a Siamese network architecture on the MNIST dataset, through which it will learn features that are specific to handwriting, such as the curves and strokes of given characters. In the next section, we will look into the architecture of the Siamese network and learn about its optimization.

Architecture

A Siamese network consists of two identical neural networks that share similar parameters, each head taking one input data point. In the middle layer, we extract similar kinds of features, as weights and biases are the same. The last layers of these networks are fed to a **contrastive loss function layer**, which calculates the similarity between the two inputs.

One question you might have is why do Siamese networks' layers share parameters? If we are already putting the effort into changing the loss function, won't it help us to train the layers separately?

There are two major reasons why we are not training layers separately:

- For every layer, we have thousands of parameters being added. Therefore, similar to how we do in a convolutional neural network approach where we share parameters, we can optimize the network faster.
- Sharing weights guarantees that two similar images won't be mapped to different locations in the feature embeddings space.

 Feature embeddings are the projection of features to some higher dimensional space, also known as the **feature embeddings space**, depending upon the task we want to achieve.

The following diagram illustrates a sample Siamese network architecture:

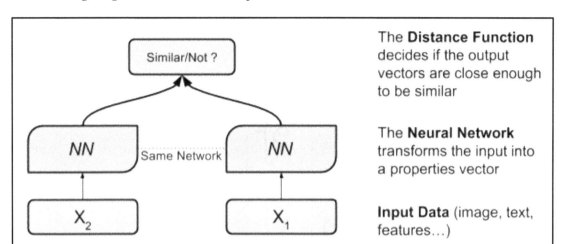

As we can see, the preceding diagram is straightforward and self-explanatory. We will now discuss the preprocessing steps required to train a Siamese network.

Preprocessing

For training a Siamese network, we need to apply a special kind of preprocessing to the dataset. While preprocessing the dataset, we have to carefully create pairs of data points as follows:

- Pairs of similar images
- Pairs of dissimilar images

The following diagram illustrates an example of a Siamese network objective for Omniglot:

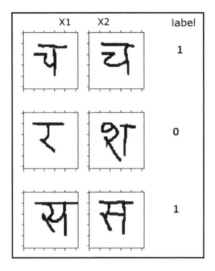

We also need to create labels accordingly for similar data points (*y=1*), and dissimilar data points (*y=0*); then, each pair is fed to the Siamese architecture. At the end of the layer, the Siamese network uses a differentiating form of the loss function to learn the differentiating features across layers. Commonly, we use just two types of function for Siamese networks—the contrastive loss function, and the triplet loss function. We will learn more about these in the next section.

Contrastive loss function

The whole idea of using Siamese architecture is not to classify between classes but to learn to discriminate between inputs. So, it requires a differentiating form of the loss function known as the **contrastive loss function**. This is given as follows:

$$L(Y, X1, X2, W) = (1 - Y) * \frac{1}{2}D_w^2 + (Y)\frac{1}{2}(max(0, m - D_w))^2$$

In this equation, $D_w = \sqrt{(f(X1) - f(X2))^2}$, $f(X)$ represents the Siamese neural network, and *m* represents the margin.

Let's solve the loss equation further. Take $Y = 1$ for similar pairs:

$$L(Y = 1) = \frac{1}{2}max(0, m - D_w)^2$$
$$D_w^2 = (f(X1) - f(X2))^2$$

If both inputs *X1* and *X2* are the same, this means that the Siamese network should be able to learn to make $D_w^2 = 0$. We add the margin *m* to the equation, so that the Siamese network doesn't make *W = 0*, in order to make D_w^2. By enforcing a margin, we ensure that the Siamese network learns a good decision boundary.

Similarly, for *Y = 0* for dissimilar pairs, this will produce the following:

$$L(Y = 0) = \frac{1}{2}D_w^2$$

Numerically speaking, for the same pair cases, the loss function becomes zero only if $D_w = 0$, otherwise it will behave like regression loss and try to learn features to ensure D_w gets close to 0.

Though the contrastive loss function is a good method for learning discriminative features, in other modified versions of the Siamese network architecture, the contrastive loss function isn't able to learn decision boundaries very clearly. In this case, we can use a new loss function known as **triplet loss**, which helps the architecture to get better results.

Triplet loss function

The triplet loss function is an alternative to the contrastive loss function. It has convergence advantages over contrastive loss functions.

To learn about the triplet loss function, first, we need to define data points in pairs as follows:

- **Anchor (A)**: The main data point
- **Positive (P)**: A data point similar to Anchor
- **Negative (N)**: A different data point than Anchor

Considering $f(X)$ is the output of Siamese networks, ideally, we can assume the following:

$$(f(A) - f(P))^2 < (f(A) - f(N))^2$$

In distance function terms, we can say the following:

$$d(A, P) - d(A, N) < 0$$

As we don't want a Siamese network to learn $f(X) = 0, X \epsilon R$, we will add the margin, similar to a contrastive loss function:

$$d(A, P) - d(A, N) + \alpha < 0$$

Using the following equations, we will define triplet loss as follows:

$$L(A, P, N) = max(0, d(A, P) - d(A, B) + \alpha)$$

The following diagram represents the triplet loss function:

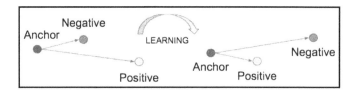

The triplet loss function converges better than the contrastive loss function because it considers three examples at a time, maintaining the distance between the **Positive** and **Negative** points as shown the preceding diagram, thereby learning decision boundaries more accurately, whereas the contrastive loss function only considers pairwise examples at a time, so in a sense, it is more greedy, which affects decision boundaries.

Applications

Often, a problem can be solved using various approaches; for example, face detection on our phones. Image classification is an approach that requires a lot of data points, whereas if we use the Siamese network architecture of one-shot learning, we can achieve greater accuracy with only a few data points. The Siamese network architecture has become one of the most popular one-shot learning architectures adopted by the software industry. It is used for various other applications, such as face detection, handwriting detection, and spam detection. But there is still a lot of scope for improvement, and various researchers are working toward this. Working on a similar theme, in the next section, we will learn about the matching networks architecture, which learns a probability distribution over labels of the training set using an attention mechanism, and different training procedures.

Understanding matching networks

Matching networks, in general, propose a framework that learns a network that maps a small training dataset and tests an unlabeled example in the same embeddings space. Matching networks aim to learn the proper embeddings representation of a small training dataset and use a differentiable kNN with a cosine similarity measure to check whether a test data point has already been seen.

Matching networks are designed to be two-fold:

- **Modeling level**: At the modeling level, they propose matching networks, which uses advances made in attention and memory that enable fast and efficient learning.
- **Training procedure**: At the training level, they have one condition—the distribution of training and test sets must be the same. For example, this could mean showing a few examples per class and switching the task from minibatch to minibatch, similar to how it will be tested when presented with a few examples of a new task.

 Matching networks incorporate the best characteristic of both parametric and non-parametric models, also famously known as differential nearest neighbor.

In the next section, we will go through the contributions made by matching networks at the modeling level, and later we will go through the training procedure contribution.

Model architecture

The matching networks architecture is majorly inspired by the attention model and memory-based networks. In all these models, a neural attention mechanism is defined to access a memory matrix, which stores useful information to solve the task at hand. To begin with, first, we need to understand certain terminologies used in matching networks:

- **Label set**: This is the sample set of all possible categories. For example, if we are using the ImageNet dataset, it consists of thousands of categories (such as cats, dogs, and birds), but as part of the label set, we will only use five of those categories.

- **Support set**: This is the sampled input data points (for example, images) of our label set categories.
- **Batch**: Similar to the support set, a batch is also a sampled set consisting of input data points of label set categories.
- *N-way k-shot method*: Here, *N* is the size of the support set, or, in simpler terms, the number of possible categories in the training set. For example, in the diagram that follows, we have four different types of dog breeds, and we are planning to use the 5-shot learning method, that is, have at least five examples of each category. This will make our matching networks architecture use *4-way 5-shot learning*, as illustrated in the following diagram:

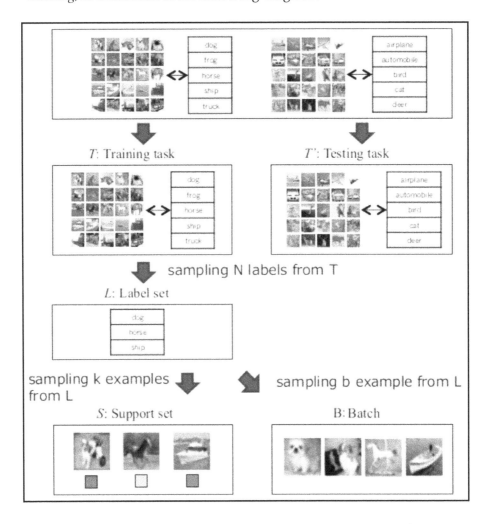

The key idea of matching networks is to map images to an embeddings space, which also encapsulates the label distribution, and then project a test image in the same embedding space using different architecture; then, later, we use cosine similarity to measure the similarity metric. Let's look at how matching networks create their embeddings space.

Training procedure

When it comes to training architecture, matching networks follow a certain technique: they try to replicate test conditions during the training phase. In simpler terms, as we have learned in the previous section, matching networks sample label sets from the training data, and later they generate a support set and a batch set from the same label set. After data preprocessing, matching networks learn their parameters by training the model to minimize the error by taking support sets as training sets, and batch sets as test sets. This training procedure of taking a support set as the training set and a batch set as the test set enables matching networks to replicate the test conditions.

In the next section, we will go through the architecture and algorithm of matching networks, and learn how to use the batch set, which is the test set, during the model's training phase.

Modeling level – the matching networks architecture

Matching networks map a support set (k examples) $S=(x_i, y_i)_{i=1}^{k}$ to a classifier $C_s(\cdot)$. Basically, matching networks define mapping $S \to C_s(\cdot)$ as a parametrized neural network $(P(\hat{y}|\hat{x}, S))$. If we talk about the simplest form of $P(\hat{y}|\hat{x}, S)$, it will be in the form of a linear combination of support set labels:

$$\hat{y} = \sum_{i=1}^{k} a(\hat{x}, x_i) y_i$$

Here, $a(\hat{x}, x_i)$ is a softmax function. If we look at it logically, we can see that $\hat{y}$ is being calculated properly in a non-parametric sense.

For example, if we have 2 classes, 0 and 1, 2 examples ($k=2$) are as follows:
$y = (0, 1)$

By turning y into one-hot encoding vectors, we will obtain the following:

$$\begin{matrix} y_1 \\ y_2 \end{matrix} = \begin{matrix} 0 & 1 \\ 1 & 0 \end{matrix}$$

Their respective kernel values are as follows:

$$a(\hat{x}, x_1) = \begin{matrix} p_{11} & p_{12} \\ p_{13} & p_{14} \end{matrix}$$

$$a(\hat{x}, x_2) = \begin{matrix} p_{21} & p_{22} \\ p_{23} & p_{24} \end{matrix}$$

By introducing the values of a and y, we will obtain the following equation:

$$\hat{y} = y_1 * a(\hat{x}, x_1) + y_2 * a(\hat{x}, x_2)$$

Upon solving this, we will obtain the following equation:

$$\hat{y} = \begin{matrix} p_{13} + p_{21} & p_{14} + p_{22} \end{matrix}$$

Overall, we can see how $\hat{y}$ turned out to be a linear combination of probabilities that determine which class the test input $\hat{x}$ belongs to. To convert any form of function into a probability space, the best choice used by the deep learning community is a softmax function, making $a(\hat{x}, x_i)$ as follows:

$$a(\hat{x}, x_i) = \frac{e^{c(f(\hat{x}), g(x_i))}}{\sum_{j=1}^{k} e^{c(f(\hat{x}), g(x_j))}}$$

Here, c is the cosine similarity function in between embeddings of the training set and test data point.

Now, the question arises as to how to extract embeddings from both the test and training sets. Any form of neural network will work. For images, the famous VGG16 or Inception Net will provide proper embeddings for both the test and train images by using transfer learning; essentially, that's what most metric-based approaches have done in the past, but weren't able to obtain human-level cognitive results.

 VGG16 and Inception Net are deep learning architectures that have given state-of-the-art results on the ImageNet dataset. They are commonly used for initial feature extraction of any image, as this will give our architecture a proper initialization for the training procedure.

Matching networks pointed out two issues with the preceding simplistic non-parametric approach:

- **Problem 1:** Embeddings of the training set images are independent of each other, without considering them to be part of a support set, even though the classification strategy, $P(\hat{y}|\hat{x}, S)$, is conditioned on the support set.

  Solution: Matching networks use a **bi-directional Long Short-Term Memory (LSTM)** to enable the encoding of each data point in the context of the whole support set. LSTMs, in general, are used to understand a sequence of data because they are able to keep context throughout data using gates inside their cells. Similarly, bi-directional LSTMs are used to enable a better understanding of the sequence of data. Matching networks use bi-directional LSTMs to ensure that embeddings for one image in the support set will have some context of all other images' embeddings.

- **Problem 2:** If we wish to calculate the similarity between two data points, we first need to bring them into the same embeddings space. So, the support set S needs to be able to contribute to extracting test image embeddings.

  Solution: Matching networks use LSTMs with read-attention over the support set S:

$$f(\hat{x}, S) = attLSTM(emeddings(\hat{x}), g(S), K)$$

Here, K is the number of unrolling steps, $emeddings(\hat{x})$ is the test image embeddings obtained through the VGG16/Inception network; and, $g(S)$ is a sample-set contribution to bring the test image embeddings into the same space.

The following diagram illustrates the matching networks architecture:

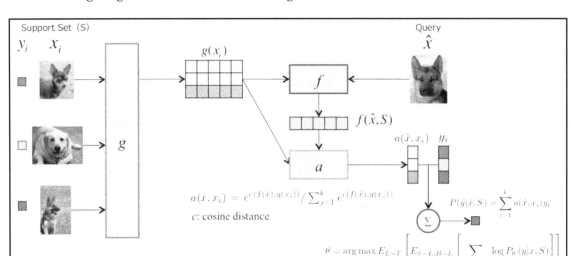

The matching networks architecture solves the problem of one-shot learning with set-to-set frameworks to replicate test conditions while training the model, as discussed in the *Training procedure* section. The matching networks' architecture has a lot of sub-parts in it. To simplify and learn it more clearly, we will go through each process from left to right:

1. As part of preprocessing data, a support set, S, of k examples will be created as $(x_i, y_i)_{i=1}^{k}$.

2. After obtaining the support set, it passes through a standard feature extraction layer (g), such as VGG or Inception.

3. Following extraction of the embeddings (the output of the g layer) of the support set (S), they are put into a bi-directional LSTM architecture. This helps the model to learn the probabilistic distribution of labels present in the support set.

4. Similar to the training set, a full-context embeddings extraction of the query image (that is, the test image) also goes through a combined bi-directional LSTM architecture, simultaneously getting contributions from $g(x_i)$ so as to map in the same embeddings space.

5. After obtaining the outputs from both architectures, the outputs are passed through the softmax layer, also known as the attention kernel step, $a(h_{k-1}, g(x_i))$.

6. The outputs obtained from $g(x_i)$ and $f'(x)$ are then used to check which category the query image belongs to:

$$\hat{y} = \sum_{i=1}^{k} a(\hat{x}, x_i) y_i$$

In this equation, $\hat{y}$ is a weighted sum of the labels in the support set.

Here, the attention kernel is a softmax function with values of cosine distance between $g(x_i)$ and $f'(x)$. To train the model, we can use any categorically-based loss function, such as the cross-entropy loss function.

 The key idea of matching networks is to create an architecture that can perform well, even for classes that are not present in the training data (that is, the support set).

Matching networks is one of the well-known approaches for one-shot learning for its innovative training procedure and fully contextual embeddings. If we try to understand the approach of matching networks in terms of human learning, it's very similar to a teaching procedure for children. To learn a new task, they are presented with a small-set series of examples, followed by a small test set, and this gets repeated. Using this procedure, and with the help of the contextual memory retention of a human brain, children learn a new task.

In the next section, we will be exploring the implementation of Siamese networks and matching networks architecture using the well-known MNIST and Omniglot datasets.

Coding exercise

In this section, we will learn about the implementation of Siamese networks and matching networks.

Let's begin with Siamese networks.

Siamese networks – the MNIST dataset

In this tutorial, we will do the following things in the order listed here:

1. Data preprocessing: Creating pairs
2. Creating a Siamese network architecture
3. Training it using the small MNIST dataset
4. Visualizing the embeddings

Perform the following steps to carry out the exercise:

1. First, import all the libraries needed using the following code:

```
# -*- encoding: utf-8 -*-
import argparse
import torch
import torchvision.datasets as dsets
import random
import numpy as np
import time
import matplotlib.pyplot as plt
from torch.autograd import Variable
from torchvision import transforms
import pickle
import torch
import torch.nn as nn
```

As we learned in the theoretical *Understanding Siamese networks* section, as part of data preprocessing, we need to create pairs:

- 1 pair-> similar; *y=1*
- 1 pair-> dissimilar; *y=0*

We are using a contrastive loss function – that's why we have just two pairs. For the triplet loss function, we'd need a different form of preprocessing.

2. To preprocess data and create an iterator for the model, first create a `Dataset` class:

```
class Dataset(object):
    '''
    Class Dataset:
    Input: numpy values
```

```
Output: torch variables.
'''
def __init__(self, x0, x1, label):
    self.size = label.shape[0]
    self.x0 = torch.from_numpy(x0)
    self.x1 = torch.from_numpy(x1)
    self.label = torch.from_numpy(label)

def __getitem__(self, index):
    return (self.x0[index],
            self.x1[index],
            self.label[index])

def __len__(self):
    return self.size
```

3. Before creating an iterator, let's create the `pairs` function and preprocess images in them:

```
def create_pairs(data, digit_indices):
    x0_data = []
    x1_data = []
    label = []
    n = min([len(digit_indices[d]) for d in range(10)]) - 1
    for d in range(10): # for MNIST dataset: as we have 10 digits
        for i in range(n):
            z1, z2 = digit_indices[d][i], digit_indices[d][i + 1]
            x0_data.append(data[z1] / 255.) # Image Preprocessing
                                            Step
            x1_data.append(data[z2] / 255.) # Image Preprocessing
                                            Step
            label.append(1)
            inc = random.randrange(1, 10)
            dn = (d + inc) % 10
            z1, z2 = digit_indices[d][i], digit_indices[dn][i]
            x0_data.append(data[z1] / 255.) # Image Preprocessing
                                            Step
            x1_data.append(data[z2] / 255.) # Image Preprocessing
                                            Step
            label.append(0)

    x0_data = np.array(x0_data, dtype=np.float32)
    x0_data = x0_data.reshape([-1, 1, 28, 28])
    x1_data = np.array(x1_data, dtype=np.float32)
    x1_data = x1_data.reshape([-1, 1, 28, 28])
    label = np.array(label, dtype=np.int32)
    return x0_data, x1_data, label
```

4. Then, create the `iterator` function. This will return a set of the given `batchsize` parameter for our training purposes:

```
def create_iterator(data, label, batchsize, shuffle=False):
    digit_indices = [np.where(label == i)[0] for i in range(10)]
    x0, x1, label = create_pairs(data, digit_indices)
    ret = Dataset(x0, x1, label)
    return ret
```

5. Then, create the `loss` function. As we know, `contrastive_loss_function` consists of two parts:

- For similar points: *(1-y)*(distance_function)^2*
- For dissimilar points: *y*{max(0,(m-distance_function^2)}*

Here, *distance_function* is taken as the Euclidean distance, also known as the **root mean square**:

```
def contrastive_loss_function(x0, x1, y, margin=1.0):
    # euclidean distance
    diff = x0 - x1
    dist_sq = torch.sum(torch.pow(diff, 2), 1)
    dist = torch.sqrt(dist_sq)
    mdist = margin - dist
    dist = torch.clamp(mdist, min=0.0)
    loss = y * dist_sq + (1 - y) * torch.pow(dist, 2)
    loss = torch.sum(loss) / 2.0 / x0.size()[0]
    return loss
```

6. Next, create the Siamese network architecture. For this, let's first create a class called `SiameseNetwork` with two functions:

- `forward_once`: In `forward_once`, the training data will pass through all layers and return the outputted embeddings.
- `forward`: In `forward`, `forward_once` will be called two times for the given input pair, and this returns a NumPy array of the embeddings obtained.

As discussed in the theory part of a Siamese network, we share parameters with both parallel layers so we don't need to explicitly create both branches—we can just create one:

```
class SiameseNetwork(nn.Module):
    def __init__(self,flag_kaf=False):
```

```
        super(SiameseNetwork, self).__init__()
        self.cnn1 = nn.Sequential(
            nn.Conv2d(1, 20, kernel_size=5),
            nn.MaxPool2d(2, stride=2),
            nn.Conv2d(20, 50, kernel_size=5),
            nn.MaxPool2d(2, stride=2))
        self.fc1 = nn.Sequential(
            nn.Linear(50 * 4 * 4, 500),
            nn.ReLU(inplace=True),
            nn.Linear(500,10),
            nn.Linear(10, 2))
    def forward_once(self, x):
        output = self.cnn1(x)
        output = output.view(output.size()[0], -1)
        output = self.fc1(output)
        return output

    def forward(self, input1, input2):
        output1 = self.forward_once(input1)
        output2 = self.forward_once(input2)
        return output1, output2
```

7. Reduce the `MNIST` dataset and choose `2000` random points, set `batchsize` as any power of 2 (for example, `128`), and import the `MNIST` dataset:

```
batchsize=128
train = dsets.MNIST(root='../data/',train=True,download=True)
test =
dsets.MNIST(root='../data/',train=False,transform=transforms.Compos
e([transforms.ToTensor(),]))
indices= np.random.choice(len(train.train_labels.numpy()), 2000,
replace=False)
indices_test= np.random.choice(len(test.test_labels.numpy()), 100,
replace=False)
```

8. We created an iterator in *step 4* – here, we will use it to create the training and test set iterators:

```
train_iter =
create_iterator(train.train_data.numpy()[indices],train.train_label
s.numpy()[indices],batchsize)
test_iter =
create_iterator(test.test_data.numpy()[indices_test],test.test_labe
ls.numpy()[indices_test],batchsize)

# call model
model = SiameseNetwork()
learning_rate = 0.01 # learning rate for optimization
```

```
momentum = 0.9 # momentum
# Loss and Optimizer
criterion = contrastive_loss_function # we will use contrastive
loss function as defined above
optimizer = torch.optim.SGD(model.parameters(),
lr=learning_rate,momentum=momentum)

# creating a train loader, and a test loader.
train_loader =
torch.utils.data.DataLoader(train_iter,batch_size=batchsize,
shuffle=True)
test_loader =
torch.utils.data.DataLoader(test,batch_size=batchsize,
shuffle=True)
```

9. Then, we train the model for a certain number of epochs and print the result:

```
train_loss = []
epochs =100
for epoch in range(epochs):
    print('Train Epoch:'+str(epoch)+"------------------>")
    for batch_idx, (x0, x1, labels) in enumerate(train_loader):
        labels = labels.float()
        x0, x1, labels = Variable(x0), Variable(x1),
        Variable(labels)
        output1, output2 = model(x0, x1)
        loss = criterion(output1, output2, labels)
        optimizer.zero_grad()
        loss.backward()
        optimizer.step()
        train_loss.append(loss.item())
        if batch_idx % batchsize == 0:
            print('Epoch: {} \tLoss: {:.6f}'.format(epoch,
                loss.item()))
```

This will give the following output:

```
Epoch: 0        Loss: 0.269623
Epoch: 1        Loss: 0.164050
Epoch: 2        Loss: 0.109350
Epoch: 3        Loss: 0.118925
Epoch: 4        Loss: 0.108258
...
...
Epoch: 97       Loss: 0.003922
Epoch: 98       Loss: 0.003155
Epoch: 99       Loss: 0.003937
```

10. Now, let's create all the functions for plotting embeddings and a loss function:

```
def plot_loss(train_loss,name="train_loss.png"):
    plt.plot(train_loss, label="train loss")
    plt.legend()
    plt.show()

def plot_mnist(numpy_all,
numpy_labels,name="./embeddings_plot.png"):
        c = ['#ff0000', '#ffff00', '#00ff00', '#00ffff', '#0000ff',
            '#ff00ff', '#990000', '#999900', '#009900', '#009999']

        for i in range(10):
            f = numpy_all[np.where(numpy_labels == i)]
            plt.plot(f[:, 0], f[:, 1], '.', c=c[i])
        plt.legend(['0', '1', '2', '3', '4', '5', '6', '7', '8',
            '9'])
        plt.savefig(name)
```

11. Plot the `loss` function using the following code:

```
plot_loss(train_loss)
```

This will give the following plot as the resultant output:

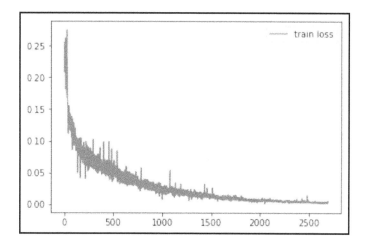

12. Then, we will define `test_model` and `testing_plots` for plotting the test set embeddings of the `MNIST` dataset:

```
def test_model(model):
        model.eval()
        all_ = []
        all_labels = []
        with torch.no_grad():
            for batch_idx, (x, labels) in enumerate(test_loader):
                x, labels = Variable(x), Variable(labels)
                output = model.forward_once(x)
                all_.extend(output.data.cpu().numpy().tolist())
all_labels.extend(labels.data.cpu().numpy().tolist())

        numpy_all = np.array(all_)
        numpy_labels = np.array(all_labels)
        return numpy_all, numpy_labels

def testing_plots(model):
        dict_pickle={}
        numpy_all, numpy_labels = test_model(model)
        dict_pickle["numpy_all"]=numpy_all
        dict_pickle["numpy_labels"]=numpy_labels
        plot_mnist(numpy_all, numpy_labels)
```

13. Then, plot `testing_plots`:

```
testing_plots(model)
```

This will give the following plot as the resultant output:

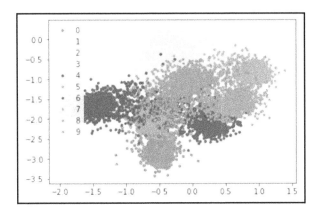

In the preceding plot, we can observe that the majority of the points are in a cluster, whereas some other points are not part of the cluster and can be seen as outliers.

Matching networks – the Omniglot dataset

In this tutorial, we will learn how to create a matching networks architecture and train it on the Omniglot dataset. To begin, let's first understand what the Omniglot dataset is.

The Omniglot dataset is designed for developing more human-like learning algorithms. It contains 1,623 different handwritten characters from 50 different alphabets. Each of the 1,623 characters was drawn online via Amazon's Mechanical Turk by 20 different people. Each image is paired with stroke data, a sequence of *[x,y,t]* coordinates with time (*t*) in milliseconds. For more details, please refer to `https://github.com/brendenlake/omniglot`.

You can download the Omniglot dataset from `https://github.com/brendenlake/omniglot`.

Our matching networks architecture implementation consists of the following five important parts (for more details, you can refer to the matching networks architecture diagram in the *Modeling level—the matching networks architecture* section):

- The embeddings extractor, *g*
- Fully contextual embeddings and the bi-directional LSTM, *f*
- The cosine similarity distance function, c
- The attention model, softmax(c)
- The loss function, cross-entropy loss

Now, we will go through each part of the matching networks and implement it:

1. Import all libraries:

```
import numpy as np
import torch
import torch.nn as nn
import math
import numpy as np
import torch.nn.functional as F
from torch.autograd import Variable
import tqdm
import torch.backends.cudnn as cudnn
from torch.optim.lr_scheduler import ReduceLROnPlateau
import matplotlib.pyplot as plt
%matplotlib inline
```

2. We will load the `omniglot` dataset, which will be transformed into `.npy` format using a helper script. In the helper script, we are just loading data in size format: *[total_number,character,28,28]* (for more details, go through the `helper.py` script available on the book's GitHub repository):

```
x = np.load('data/data.npy') # Load Data
x = np.reshape(x, newshape=(x.shape[0], x.shape[1], 28, 28, 1)) #
expand dimension from (x.shape[0],x.shape[1],28,28)
np.random.shuffle(x) # shuffle dataset
x_train, x_val, x_test = x[:1200], x[1200:1411], x[1411:] # divide
dataset in to train, val,ctest
batch_size = 16 # setting batch_size
n_classes = x.shape[0] # total number of classes
classes_per_set = 20 # Number of classes per set
samples_per_class = 1 # as we are choosing it to be one shot
learning, so we have 1 sample
```

If you wish to learn more about data-loading methods, you can refer to the `helper.py` file available on GitHub at `https://github.com/PacktPublishing/Hands-On-One-shot-Learning-with-Python/tree/master/Chapter02`.

3. Preprocess the images using the normalization method:

```
def processes_batch(data, mu, sigma):
    return (data - mu) / sigma

# Normalize Dataset
x_train = processes_batch(x_train, np.mean(x_train),
np.std(x_train))
x_val = processes_batch(x_val, np.mean(x_val), np.std(x_val))
x_test = processes_batch(x_test, np.mean(x_test), np.std(x_test))

# Defining dictionary of dataset
datatset = {"train": x_train, "val": x_val, "test": x_test}
```

4. Now, run the following code to visualize the 0th example of one character written by 20 people:

```
temp = x_train[0,:,:,:,:]
for i in range(0,20):
    plt.figure()
    plt.imshow(temp[i,:,:,0])
```

By running the preceding code, you will obtain 20 of the following:

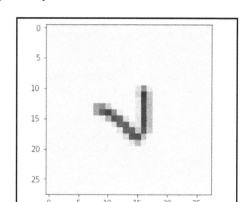

Next, we will perform some processing on the training data.

To load the Omniglot dataset and prepare it for use in the matching networks architecture, we need to create the following:

- The label set: choose_label
- The support set: support_set_x, support_set_y
- A batch from the support set examples

We will perform the following steps:

1. First, create a batch that can give a support set and a target set:

```
def sample_batch(data):
    """
    Generates sample batch
    :param : data - one of(train,test,val) our current dataset
    shape [total_classes,20,28,28,1]
    :return: [support_set_x,support_set_y,target_x,target_y]
    for Matching Networks
    """
    support_set_x = np.zeros((batch_size, classes_per_set,
        samples_per_class, data.shape[2], data.shape[3],
        data.shape[4]), np.float32)
    support_set_y = np.zeros((batch_size, classes_per_set,
        samples_per_class), np.int32)
    target_x = np.zeros((batch_size, data.shape[2],
        data.shape[3], data.shape[4]), np.float32)
    target_y = np.zeros((batch_size, 1), np.int32)
```

```
            for i in range(batch_size):
                choose_classes = np.random.choice(data.shape[0],
                    size=classes_per_set, replace=False) # choosing
                    random classes
                choose_label = np.random.choice(classes_per_set,
                    size=1) # label set
                choose_samples = np.random.choice(data.shape[1],
                    size=samples_per_class + 1, replace=False)
                x_temp = data[choose_classes] # choosing classes
                x_temp = x_temp[:, choose_samples] # choosing sample
                    batch from classes chosen outputs 20X2X28X28X1
                y_temp = np.arange(classes_per_set) # will return
                    [0,1,2,3,...,19]
                support_set_x[i] = x_temp[:, :-1]
                support_set_y[i] = np.expand_dims(y_temp[:],
                    axis=1) # expand dimension
                target_x[i] = x_temp[choose_label, -1]
                target_y[i] = y_temp[choose_label]
            return support_set_x, support_set_y, target_x, target_y
                # returns support of [batch_size, 20 classes per set,
                1 sample, 28, 28,1]
    def get_batch(dataset_name):
            """
            gen batch while training
            :param dataset_name: The name of dataset(one of
            "train","val","test")
            :return: a batch images
            """
            support_set_x, support_set_y, target_x, target_y =
            sample_batch(datatset[dataset_name])
            support_set_x =
            support_set_x.reshape((support_set_x.shape[0],
                support_set_x.shape[1] * support_set_x.shape[2],
                support_set_x.shape[3], support_set_x.shape[4],
                support_set_x.shape[5]))
            support_set_y =
            support_set_y.reshape(support_set_y.shape[0],
                support_set_y.shape[1] * support_set_y.shape[2])
            return support_set_x, support_set_y, target_x, target_y
```

If you recall, in matching networks architecture, there are four main parts of the network:

- The embeddings extractor (g)
- Full-context embeddings (f)
- The attention model (a)
- The distance function (c)

2. Create a classifier:

```python
def convLayer(in_channels, out_channels, dropout_prob=0.0):
    """
    :param dataset_name: The name of dataset(one of
    "train","val","test")
    :return: a batch images
    """
    cnn_seq = nn.Sequential(
        nn.Conv2d(in_channels, out_channels, 3, 1, 1),
        nn.ReLU(True),
        nn.BatchNorm2d(out_channels),
        nn.MaxPool2d(kernel_size=2, stride=2),
        nn.Dropout(dropout_prob)
    )
    return cnn_seq

class Embeddings_extractor(nn.Module):
    def __init__(self, layer_size=64, num_channels=1,
        dropout_prob=0.5, image_size=28):
        super(Embeddings_extractor, self).__init__()
        """
        Build a CNN to produce embeddings
        :param layer_size:64(default)
        :param num_channels:
        :param keep_prob:
        :param image_size:
        """
        self.layer1 = convLayer(num_channels, layer_size,
            dropout_prob)
        self.layer2 = convLayer(layer_size, layer_size,
            dropout_prob)
        self.layer3 = convLayer(layer_size, layer_size,
            dropout_prob)
        self.layer4 = convLayer(layer_size, layer_size,
            dropout_prob)

        finalSize = int(math.floor(image_size / (2 * 2 * 2 * 2)))
        self.outSize = finalSize * finalSize * layer_size

    def forward(self, image_input):
        """
        :param: Image
        :return: embeddings
        """
        x = self.layer1(image_input)
        x = self.layer2(x)
        x = self.layer3(x)
```

```
x = self.layer4(x)
x = x.view(x.size()[0], -1)
return x
```

3. Create an attention model after the classifier. $a(x, \hat{x})=$ the softmax of cosine similarities:

```
class AttentionalClassify(nn.Module):
    def __init__(self):
        super(AttentionalClassify, self).__init__()
    def forward(self, similarities, support_set_y):
        """
        Products pdfs over the support set classes for the target
        set image.
        :param similarities: A tensor with cosine similarites of
        size[batch_size, sequence_length]
        :param support_set_y: [batch_size, sequence_length,
        classes_num]
        :return: Softmax pdf shape[batch_size, classes_num]
        """
        softmax = nn.Softmax(dim=1)
        softmax_similarities = softmax(similarities)
        preds = softmax_similarities.unsqueeze(1).
        bmm(support_set_y).squeeze()
        return preds
```

4. Create a distance network, which will take the output from the test image and training embeddings to calculate the distance. Find the cosine similarities between the support set and `input_test_image`:

```
class DistanceNetwork(nn.Module):
    def __init__(self):
        super(DistanceNetwork, self).__init__()

    def forward(self, support_set, input_image):
        eps = 1e-10
        similarities = []
        for support_image in support_set:
            sum_support = torch.sum(torch.pow(support_image, 2), 1)
            support_manitude = sum_support.clamp(eps,
                float("inf")).rsqrt()
            dot_product = input_image.unsqueeze(1).
                bmm(support_image.unsqueeze(2)).squeeze()
            cosine_similarity = dot_product * support_manitude
            similarities.append(cosine_similarity)
        similarities = torch.stack(similarities)
        return similarities.t()
```

5. Create `BidirectionalLSTM`, which will take input and output from the test image, and put them in the same embeddings space. If we wish to use full-context embeddings, matching networks has introduced a bi-directional LSTM for that:

```
class BidirectionalLSTM(nn.Module):
    def __init__(self, layer_size, batch_size, vector_dim):
        super(BidirectionalLSTM, self).__init__()
        self.batch_size = batch_size
        self.hidden_size = layer_size[0]
        self.vector_dim = vector_dim
        self.num_layer = len(layer_size)
        self.lstm = nn.LSTM(input_size=self.vector_dim,
            num_layers=self.num_layer,
            hidden_size=self.hidden_size, bidirectional=True)
        self.hidden = (Variable(torch.zeros(
            self.lstm.num_layers * 2, self.batch_size,
            self.lstm.hidden_size),requires_grad=False),
            Variable(torch.zeros(self.lstm.num_layers * 2,
            self.batch_size, self.lstm.hidden_size),
            requires_grad=False))

    def repackage_hidden(self,h):
        """Wraps hidden states in new Variables,
        to detach them from their history."""
        if type(h) == torch.Tensor:
            return Variable(h.data)
        else:
            return tuple(self.repackage_hidden(v) for v in h)
    def forward(self, inputs):
        self.hidden = self.repackage_hidden(self.hidden)
        output, self.hidden = self.lstm(inputs, self.hidden)
        return output
```

6. Let's now club all the small modules we have made and create a matching network:

```
class MatchingNetwork(nn.Module):
    def __init__(self, keep_prob, batch_size=32, num_channels=1,
    learning_rate=1e-3, fce=False, num_classes_per_set=20,
    num_samples_per_class=1, image_size=28):
        super(MatchingNetwork, self).__init__()
        self.batch_size = batch_size
        self.keep_prob = keep_prob
        self.num_channels = num_channels
        self.learning_rate = learning_rate
        self.num_classes_per_set = num_classes_per_set
```

```python
            self.num_samples_per_class = num_samples_per_class
            self.image_size = image_size
            # Let's set all peices of Matching Networks Architecture
            self.g = Embeddings_extractor(layer_size=64,
                num_channels=num_channels, dropout_prob=keep_prob,
                image_size=image_size)
            self.f = fce # if we are considering full-context
                        embeddings
            self.c = DistanceNetwork() # cosine distance among
                        embeddings
            self.a = AttentionalClassify() # softmax of cosine
                        distance of embeddings
            if self.f: self.lstm = BidirectionalLSTM(layer_size=[32],
                batch_size=self.batch_size, vector_dim=self.g.outSize)

    def forward(self, support_set_images, support_set_y_one_hot,
    target_image, target_y):
            # produce embeddings for support set images
            encoded_images = []
            for i in np.arange(support_set_images.size(1)):
                gen_encode = self.g(support_set_images[:, i, :, :])
                encoded_images.append(gen_encode)
            # produce embeddings for target images
            gen_encode = self.g(target_image)
            encoded_images.append(gen_encode)
            output = torch.stack(encoded_images,dim=0)
            # if we are considering full-context embeddings
            if self.f:
                output = self.lstm(output)
            # get similarities between support set embeddings and
            target
            similarites = self.c(support_set=output[:-1],
            input_image=output[-1])
            # produce predictions for target probabilities
            preds = self.a(similarites,
support_set_y=support_set_y_one_hot)
            # calculate the accuracy
            values, indices = preds.max(1)
            accuracy = torch.mean((indices.squeeze() ==
target_y).float())
            crossentropy_loss = F.cross_entropy(preds, target_y.long())

            return accuracy, crossentropy_loss
```

7. Create a dataset loader. For our case, as we are using the Omniglot dataset, it will create an Omniglot builder that calls the matching network and runs its epochs for training, testing, and validation purposes:

```
def run_epoch(total_train_batches, name='train'):
    """
    Run the training epoch
    :param total_train_batches: Number of batches to train on
    :return:
    """
    total_c_loss = 0.0
    total_accuracy = 0.0
    for i in range(int(total_train_batches)):
            x_support_set, y_support_set, x_target, y_target =
                get_batch(name)
            x_support_set = Variable(
                torch.from_numpy(x_support_set)).float()
            y_support_set =
    Variable(torch.from_numpy(y_support_set),
                requires_grad=False).long()
            x_target = Variable(torch.from_numpy(x_target)).float()
            y_target = Variable(torch.from_numpy(y_target),
                requires_grad=False).squeeze().long()

            # convert to one hot encoding
            y_support_set = y_support_set.unsqueeze(2)
            sequence_length = y_support_set.size()[1]
            batch_size = y_support_set.size()[0]
            y_support_set_one_hot = Variable(
                torch.zeros(batch_size, sequence_length,
                classes_per_set).scatter_(2,
                y_support_set.data,1), requires_grad=False)

            # reshape channels and change order
            size = x_support_set.size()
            x_support_set = x_support_set.permute(0, 1, 4, 2, 3)
            x_target = x_target.permute(0, 3, 1, 2)
            acc, c_loss = matchNet(x_support_set,
                y_support_set_one_hot, x_target, y_target)

            # optimize process
            optimizer.zero_grad()
            c_loss.backward()
            optimizer.step()

            iter_out = "tr_loss: {}, tr_accuracy:
                {}".format(c_loss, acc)
            total_c_loss += c_loss
```

```
                total_accuracy += acc

        total_c_loss = total_c_loss / total_train_batches
        total_accuracy = total_accuracy / total_train_batches
        return total_c_loss, total_accuracy
```

8. Set up the experiment variables:

```
batch_size=20
num_channels=1
lr=1e-3
image_size=28
classes_per_set=20
samples_per_class=1
keep_prob=0.0
fce=True
optim="adam"
wd=0
matchNet = MatchingNetwork(keep_prob, batch_size, num_channels, lr,
    fce, classes_per_set, samples_per_class, image_size)
total_iter = 0
total_train_iter = 0
optimizer = torch.optim.Adam(matchNet.parameters(), lr=lr,
    weight_decay=wd)
scheduler = ReduceLROnPlateau(optimizer, 'min',verbose=True)

# Training setup
total_epochs = 100
total_train_batches = 10
total_val_batches = 5
total_test_batches = 5
```

9. Now, run the experiments:

```
train_loss,train_accuracy=[],[]
val_loss,val_accuracy=[],[]
test_loss,test_accuracy=[],[]


for e in range(total_epochs):
    ############################ Training Step
########################################
    total_c_loss, total_accuracy =
        run_epoch(total_train_batches,'train')
    train_loss.append(total_c_loss)
    train_accuracy.append(total_accuracy)
    ############################ Validation Step
########################################
```

```
total_val_c_loss, total_val_accuracy =
    run_epoch(total_val_batches, 'val')
val_loss.append(total_val_c_loss)
val_accuracy.append(total_val_accuracy)
print("Epoch {}: train_loss:{:.2f} train_accuracy:{:.2f}
    valid_loss:{:.2f} valid_accuracy:{:.2f}".format(e,
    total_c_loss, total_accuracy, total_val_c_loss,
    total_val_accuracy))
```

After running this code block, you will see the model start the training and print the following output:

```
Epoch 0: train_loss:2.99 train_accuracy:0.11 valid_loss:2.98
valid_accuracy:0.22
Epoch 1: train_loss:2.97 train_accuracy:0.20 valid_loss:2.97
valid_accuracy:0.28
Epoch 2: train_loss:2.95 train_accuracy:0.31 valid_loss:2.94
valid_accuracy:0.37
```

10. Now, let's obtain our test accuracy by running the following code block:

```
total_test_c_loss, total_test_accuracy =
run_epoch(total_test_batches,'test')
print("test_accuracy:{}%".format(total_test_accuracy*100))
```

After running this code block, you will see the following output:

```
test_accuracy:86.0%
```

11. Let's visualize our results:

```
def plot_loss(train,val,name1="train_loss",name2="val_loss"):
    plt.plot(train, label=name1)
    plt.plot(val, label=name2)
    plt.legend()

plot_loss(train_loss,val_loss)
```

After running these cells, you will see plots like these:

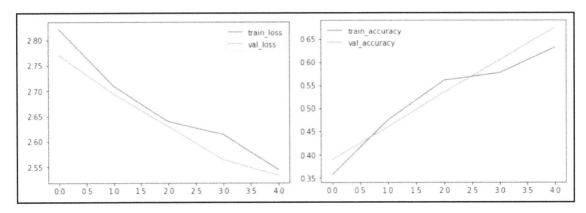

In this section, we have explored the implementations of Siamese networks using the MNIST dataset, and of the matching network architecture using the Omniglot dataset. In the Siamese network coding exercise, we created a small convolutional layer that was extended by a fully connected layer sister architecture. After training the model, we also plotted the two-dimensional embeddings obtained by the model and observed how certain numbers are clustered together. Similarly, in the matching networks coding exercise, we implemented small architectures of every module of matching networks, such as an embeddings extractor, an attention model, and fully contextual embeddings. We also observed that with only 100 epochs, we were able to attain ~86% accuracy and plotted the accuracy and loss graph for the matching network architecture.

You may have also observed that certain models were trained from scratch – we could have used transfer learning architectures, or increased the hidden size of the LSTM architecture, or perhaps considered a weighted cross-entropy loss function. There is always room for experiments and improvement. If you wish to experiment further with this model, I suggest you visit the GitHub page for this book.

Summary

In this chapter, we learned about metrics-based, one-shot learning methods. We explored two neural network architectures that have been used for one-shot learning in both the research community and software industry as well. We also learned how to evaluate trained models. Then, we executed an exercise in Siamese networks using the MNIST dataset. In conclusion, we can say that both the matching networks and Siamese network architectures have successfully proven that by changing the loss function or feature representation, we can achieve our objective with a limited amount of data.

In the next chapter, we will be exploring different optimization-based methods and learn how they differ from metrics-based methods.

Questions

1. What are similarity metrics? Why does cosine similarity work best?
2. Why do matching networks use the LSTM architecture to obtain embeddings?
3. What are the disadvantages associated with the contrastive loss function, and how does the triplet loss function assist in solving it?
4. What is the curse of dimensionality? How can we deal with it?

Further reading

To get into more depth on the architectures covered in this chapter, to explore how and why they work, read the following papers:

- *Siamese Neural Networks for One-Shot Image Recognition* (https://www.cs.cmu.edu/~rsalakhu/papers/oneshot1.pdf)
- *Matching Networks for One Shot Learning* (https://arxiv.org/pdf/1606.04080.pdf)

3
Model-Based Methods

In the last chapter, we discussed two optimization-based methods. We attempted to train models with a *learn to learn* mechanism, similar to what is seen in humans. Of course, apart from the ability to learn new things, humans also have access to a large amount of memory when performing any task. This enables us to learn a new task more easily by recalling past memories and experiences. Following the same thought process, model-based architecture is designed with the addition of external memory for the rapid generalization of one-shot learning tasks. In these approaches, models converge with only a few training steps using information stored in external memory.

The following topics will be covered in this chapter:

- Understanding Neural Turing Machines
- Memory-augmented neural networks
- Meta networks
- Coding exercises

Technical requirements

You will require the Python, Anaconda, Jupyter Notebook, PyTorch, and Matplotlib libraries to learn and execute the project in this chapter.

You can find the code files for this chapter in the GitHub repository of this book at `https:/ /github.com/PacktPublishing/Hands-On-One-shot-Learning-with-Python`.

Understanding Neural Turing Machines

During the early days of AI, the field was heavily dominated by a symbolic approach to processing. In other words, it relied on processing information with symbols and structures, as well as rules to manipulate them. It wasn't until the 1980s when the field of AI took a different approach—connectionism. The most promising modeling technique of connectionism is neural networks; however, they are often met with two heavy criticisms:

- Neural networks accept inputs of a fixed size only, which won't be of much help in real life where inputs are of variable length.
- Neural networks are unable to bind values to specific locations within data structures that are heavily employed by the two information systems we know of—the human brain and computers. In simpler terms, in neural networks, we can't set specific weights into specific locations.

The first problem can be resolved by RNNs that have achieved state-of-the-art performance on various tasks. The second problem can be resolved by looking at **Neural Turing Machines** (**NTMs**). In this section, we will discuss the overall architecture of an NTM, which is foundational to understanding **memory-augmented neural networks** (**MANNs**) that modify the NMT's architecture and adapt it for a one-shot learning task.

Architecture of an NTM

Modern computers have evolved a lot over the past 50 years; however, they are still composed of three systems—memory, control flow, and arithmetic/logic operations. Research from the fields of biology and computational neuroscience provide extensive evidence that memory is crucial in the quick and meaningful storage and retrieval of information. Taking inspiration from this, an NTM is fundamentally composed of a neural network, consisting of a controller and a two-dimensional matrix called the memory bank (or memory matrix). At each time step, the neural network receives some input and generates output corresponding to that input. In the process of doing so, it also accesses the internal memory bank and performs read and/or write operations on it. Drawing inspiration from traditional Turing machines, NMT uses the term **head** to specify memory location. The overall architecture is shown in the following figure:

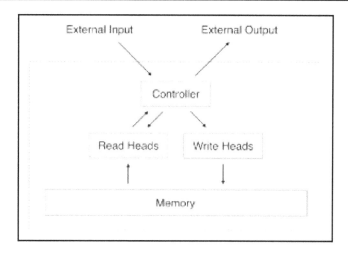

The overall architecture looks good; however, there's one problem with this. If we access the memory location by specifying the row and column index in the memory matrix, we can't take the gradient of that index. This operation is not back-propagable and would restrict the training of NMT using standard back-propagation and gradient-descent-based optimization techniques. To resolve this problem, the controller of the NTM interacts with memory using *blurry* read and write operations that interact with all elements of the memory to varying degrees. More precisely, the controller produces weights over all the memory locations in a differential manner, which helps in training the network from end to end using standard gradient-based optimization methods.

In the next section, we will discuss how these weights are produced and how read and write operations are performed.

Modeling

The memory matrix at time step t (M_t) has R rows and C columns. There's an attention mechanism that dictates which memory location the attention head should read from/write to. This attention vector, generated by the controller is a *length-R* vector, called the **weight vector** (w_t), where each entry of this vector $w_t(i)$ is the weight for the ith row of the memory bank. The weight vector is normalized, which means it satisfies the following conditions:

$$0 \leq w_t(i) \leq 1$$

$$\sum_{i=1}^{R} w_t(i)Z = 1$$

Reading

The read head will return a *length-C* vector, r_t, that is a linear combination of the memory's rows $M_t(i)$ scaled by the weight vector:

$$r_t \leftarrow \sum_i^R w_t(i)M_t(i)$$

Writing

Writing is a combination of two steps: erasing and adding. In order to erase old data, the write head uses an additional length-C erase vector, e_t, along with the weight vector. The following equations define the intermediate step of erasing the rows:

$$M_t^{erased}(i) \leftarrow M_{t-1}(i)[\mathbf{1} - w_t(i)e_t]$$

Finally, the write head uses a *length-C* add vector, a_t, along with M^{erased} from the preceding equation and a weight vector to update the rows of the memory matrix:

$$M_t(i) \leftarrow M_t^{erased} + w_t(i)a_t$$

Addressing

The key to the read and write operations is the weight vector, which indicates which rows to read from/write to. The controller produces this weight vector in four stages. Each stage produces an intermediate vector that gets passed to the next stage:

- The first stage is content-based addressing, the goal of which is to generate a weight vector based on how similar each row is to the given key vector, k_t, of length C. More precisely, the controller emits vector k_t that is compared to each row of M_t using a cosine similarity measure, defined as follows:

$$K(u, v) = \frac{u \cdot v}{||u|| \cdot ||v||}$$

The content weight vector is not normalized yet, so it is normalized with the following operation:

$$w_t^c(i) = \frac{exp\Big(\beta_t K(k_t, M_t(i))\Big)}{\sum_j exp\Big(\beta_t K(k_t, M_t(j))\Big)}$$

- The second stage is the location-based addressing, which focuses on reading/writing from specific memory locations as opposed to location values done during stage 1. Following that, a scalar parameter, $g_t \in (0,1)$, called the interpolation gate, blends the content weight vector, w_t^c, with the previous time step's weight vector, w_{t-1}, to produce the gated weighting, w_t^g. This allows the system to learn when to use (or ignore) content-based addressing:

$$w_t^g \leftarrow g_t w_t^c + (1 - g_t)w_{t-1}$$

- In the third stage, after interpolation, the head emits a normalized shift weighting, s_t, to perform a shift modulo R operation (that is, move rows upward or downward). This is defined by the following operation:

$$\tilde{w}_t(i) \leftarrow \sum_{j=0}^{R-1} w_t^g(j) s_t(i - j)$$

- The fourth and final stage, sharpening, is used to prevent the shifted weight, $\tilde{w}_t$, from blurring. This is done using a scalar $\gamma \geq 1$ and applying the following operation:

$$w_t(i) \leftarrow \frac{\tilde{w}_t(i)^{\gamma_t}}{\sum_j \tilde{w}_t(j)^{\gamma_t}}$$

All the operations, including reading, writing, and the four stages of addressing, are differential, and thus the entire NMT model could be trained from end to end with back-propagation and any gradient-descent-based optimizer. The controller is a neural network that could be a feed-forward network or even a recurrent neural network, such as a **long short-term memory (LSTM)**. It has been shown to achieve good performance at various algorithmic tasks, such as the copy task, which will be implemented later in the chapter.

Now that we understand the architecture and the working of NTMs, we are ready to dive into MANNs, which are a modification of NMTs and have been modified to excel at one-shot learning.

Memory-augmented neural networks

The goal of MANNs is to excel at one-shot learning tasks. The NMT controller, as we read earlier, uses both content-based addressing and location-based addressing. On the other hand, the MANN controller uses only content-based addressing. There are two reasons for this. One reason is that location-based addressing is not required for one-shot learning tasks. In this task, for a given input, there are only two actions that a controller might need to take and both actions are content dependent and not location dependent. One action is taken when the input is very similar to a previously seen input, in which case we can update the current contents of the memory. The other action is taken when the current input is not similar to previously seen inputs, in which case we don't want to overwrite the recent information; instead, we write to the least-used memory location. The memory module, in this case, is called the **least recently used access** (**LRUA**) module.

Reading

The read operation of MANNs is very similar to the read operation of NTMs, with a minor difference being that the weight vector here uses only content-based addressing (stage -1 of NMT addressing). More precisely, the controller uses a normalized read weight vector, w_t^r, which is used along with the rows of the M_t to produce the read vector, r_t:

$$r_t \leftarrow \sum_i^R w_t^r(i) M_t(i)$$

The read-weight vector, w_t^r, is produced by a controller that is defined by the following operations:

$$w_t^r = \frac{exp\Big(K(k_t, M_t(i))\Big)}{\sum_j exp\Big(K(k_t, M_t(j))\Big)}$$

Here, operation *K()* is the cosine similarity, similar to the one defined for NMTs.

Writing

To write into the memory, the controller interpolates between writing to the most recently read memory rows and writing to the least recently read memory rows.

$$M_t(i) \leftarrow M_{t-1}(i) + w_t^w(i)k_t$$
$$w_t^u \leftarrow \gamma w_{t-1}^u + w_t^r + w_t^w$$

MANNs have shown promising results with a one-shot classification task on Omniglot datasets. They perform well because of their underlying model NTMs. NTMs are capable of rapidly encoding, storing, and retrieving data. They are also capable of storing both long-term and short-term weights. An NTM can be added with a MANN's approach of keeping track of the *least recently used memory location* to perform content-based addressing for reading and write to the *least recently used* location. It makes MANN a perfect candidate for few-shot learning.

In the next section, we will learn another model-based architecture, which consists of four networks in architecture, and has made a significant contribution to the one-shot learning domain.

Understanding meta networks

Meta networks, as the name suggests, are a form of the model-based meta-learning approach. In usual deep-learning methods, weights of neural networks are updated by stochastic gradient descent, which takes a lot of time to train. As we know, the stochastic gradient descent approach means that we will consider each training data point for a weight update, so if our batch size is 1, this will lead to a very slow optimization of the model—in other words, a **slow weights** update.

Meta networks suggest a solution to the problem of slow weights by training a neural network in parallel to the original neural network to predict the parameters of an objective task. The generated weights are called **fast weights**. If you recall, LSTM meta-learners (see `Chapter 4`, *Optimization-Based Methods*) are also built on similar grounds to predict parameter updates of a task using an LSTM cell.

Similar to other meta-learning approaches, meta networks consist of two levels:

- **Meta-learner**: The meta-learner acquires generic knowledge of different tasks. In the meta network's case, this is an embeddings function, which is used to compare features of two different data points.
- **Base-learner**: The base-learner attempts to learn a targeted task (a task objective network could be a simple classifier).

 The goal of a meta-level learner is to acquire a general knowledge of different tasks. The knowledge can then be transferred to the base-level learner to provide generalization in the context of a single task.

As discussed, meta networks learn two forms of weights: slow weights and fast weights. To learn those weights for both a meta-learner (embeddings function) and base-learner (classification model), we need two different networks. This makes meta networks one of the most complex networks we have covered in this book so far. In short, meta networks consist of four types of neural networks, with their respective parameters to train. In the next section, we will go through every network present inside meta networks and learn about their architecture.

Algorithm of meta networks

To begin learning about meta networks, we first need to define the following terms:

- **Support set**: Sampled input data points (x,y) from the training set.
- **Test set**: Sampled data points (x,y) from the training set.
- **Embedding function** (f_θ): As part of a meta-learner, the *embedding function* is very similar to Siamese networks. It is trained to predict whether two inputs are of the same class.
- **Base-learner model** (g_ϕ): A base-learner model attempts to complete the actual learning task (for example, a classification model).
- θ^+: Fast weights of the embeddings function, (f_θ).
- ϕ^+: Fast weights of the base-learner model, (g_ϕ).
- F_w: An LSTM architecture for learning the fast weights, θ, of the embedding function, (f_θ), of a slow network.
- G_v: A neural network parameterized by v learning fast weights, ϕ, for the base learner, g_ϕ, from its loss gradients.

The following diagram illustrates a meta-network architecture:

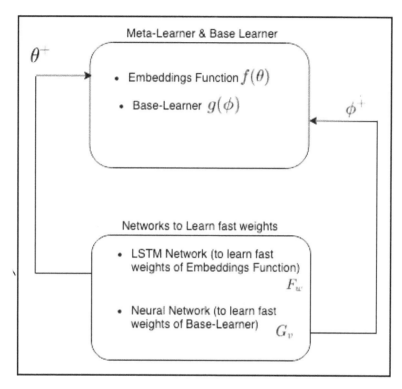

As we can see in the diagram, meta-learners base learners consist of slow weights, (θ, ϕ). To learn fast weights, (θ^+, ϕ^+), meta networks use two different networks:

- LSTM networks, (F_w), to learn the embedding function's (meta-learner) fast weights—that is, θ^+.
- Neural networks (G_v) to learn the base learner's fast weights, that is, ϕ^+.

Now that we have learned about the concept and architecture of fast and slow weights, let's try to observe the meta networks architecture as a whole:

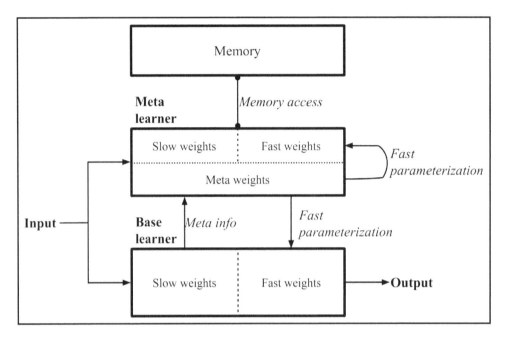

As we can see in the preceding diagram, meta networks consist of a base learner and a meta-learner (an embeddings function) that is equipped with *external memory*. We can also see fast-parameterization arrows going in to both the meta-learner and the base learner; those are the output from the meta weights, which consist of models used for learning fast weights.

Now let's go through a simple description of training. As training input data comes, it passes through both the meta-learner and base learner. In the meta-learner, it is used for continuous learning (updating parameters), whereas in the base learner, after preprocessing the input, it passes *meta info* (*gradients*) to the meta-learner. After this, the meta-learner, using *meta info* (*gradients*), returns fast a parameterization update to the base learner to optimize by using an integration of slow and fast weights (as shown in the following diagram). The underlying key idea of meta networks is to learn weights in a fast manner for rapid generalizations by processing *meta information*.

In MetaNet, the learner's loss gradients are *meta information of* the task. There is one more important question of MetaNet: how can it use both fast weights and slow weights to make a prediction?

In MetaNet, slow and fast weights are combined to make predictions in neural networks, as shown in the following diagram. Here, $\oplus$ means the element-wise sum:

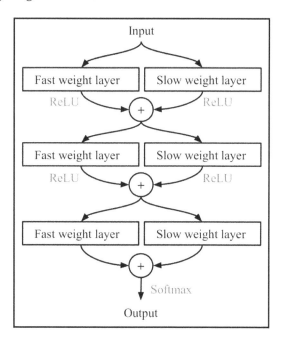

In the next section, we will go through a step-by-step description of the algorithm, the extraction of meta information, and the final model prediction.

Algorithm

Meta networks also follow a similar training procedure to that of matching networks. Here training data is divided into two types: the support set, S = (x'_i, y'_i) and the test set, U = (x_i, y_i).

Remember that at present, we have four networks, $(f(\theta), g(\phi), F_w, G_v)$, and four sets of model parameters to learn, (θ, ϕ, w, v). Let's go through all of the steps of the algorithm:

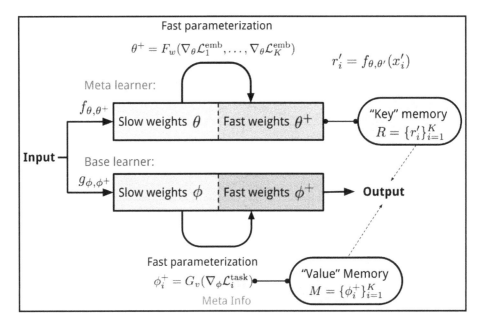

Following are the steps of the algorithm:

1. Sample K random pairs from support the set, S.

    For $t = 1, \ldots, K$:

    - Forward pass the data point through the embeddings function $f(\theta)$.
    - Calculate the cross-entropy loss, ($L_{embeddings}$).

2. Forward pass the data through the LSTM network to calculate θ^+:
    $\theta^+ = F_w(\nabla L_{embeddings})$.

3. Next, go through the examples in the support set, S, and calculate the fast weights for each example. Simultaneously, update the external memory with the embeddings that you obtained.

For $i = 1, \ldots, K$:

- Forward pass the base learner, $g_\phi(x_i)$ (for example, the classification model), and calculate the loss function, L_i^{task} (for example, cross-entropy).
- Calculate the base-learner gradients, ∇L_i^{task}, and use them to compute the example-level fast weights, $\phi_i^+ = G_v(\nabla L_i^{task})$.
- Store calculated fast weights for the base learner, ϕ_i^+, at the ith location of the *value* part of the memory, M.
- Merge fast and slow weights using $\oplus$ in the embeddings network.
- Forward pass the support sample through the embeddings network and obtain the embeddings, $r_i' = f_{\theta,\theta^+}(x_i')$.
- Store r_i' at the ith location of the *key* part of the memory, R.

4. Lastly, it is time to construct the training loss using the test set, U=(x_i, y_i). Begin with $L_{train} = 0$.

   For $j = 1, \ldots, L$:

   - Forward pass the test sample through the embeddings network and obtain the test embeddings, $r_j = f_{\theta,\theta^+}(x_j)$.
   - Calculate the similarity between the support set's stored embeddings, R, and the obtained embeddings, r_j. You can do this by using $a_j = Cosine(R, r_j)$. Here, R refers to the data stored in the external memory.
   - Now, calculate the fast weights of the base learner (ϕ^+) by using the fast weights of the support set samples (M). You can do this by using $\phi_j^+ = softmax(a_j)^T M$. Here, M refers to the data stored in the external memory.
   - Forward pass the test sample through the base learner using the latest ϕ^+, and calculate the loss function, L_i^{task}.
   - Update the training loss using $L_{train} \leftarrow L_{train} + L^{task}(g_{\phi,\phi^+}(x_i), y_i)$.

5. Update all the parameters (θ,φ,w,v) using L_{train}.

When it comes to the choice of the embeddings network, meta networks use the LSTM architecture. As we have seen, matching the networks and LSTM meta-learners also follows the same strategy used to extract the contextual embeddings of data and meta information respectively. It's because of the LSTM architecture's tendency to remember history that enables the objective of the meta-learner to extract important information across tasks.

For example, say we are training our network for multiple tasks, such as cat breed classification and dog breed classification. When we train using an LSTM meta-learner, it learns the strategy of weight updates in, say, dog breed classification, and uses this learned information to optimize its operations for cat breed classification using a few steps and less data. Using meta networks achieved 95.92% accuracy on the Omniglot dataset, whereas human accuracy is only 95.5%, and therefore meta networks are considered one of the state-of-the-art models.

Coding exercises

In this section, we will first go through the implementation of NTMs and later go through MAANs using the Omniglot dataset. So, let's begin!

 Some parts of the code aren't included as part of this exercise. If you wish to get a runnable code, please take a look at this book's GitHub repository at `https://github.com/PacktPublishing/Hands-On-One-shot-Learning-with-Python`.

Implementation of NTM

As discussed, an NTM is composed of two important components:

- A neural network, also known as the controller
- A two-dimensional matrix called memory

In this tutorial, we will implement a simplistic version of both and try to showcase the copy tasks.

The task objective is as follows:

- The NTM model is shown a random k-dimensional vector for T time steps.
- The job of the network is to output these T k-dimensional random vectors from zero vectors at each time step.

Perform the following steps to implement NTMs:

1. First, import all the required libraries:

```
import torch
from torch import nn
import torch.nn.functional as F
import numpy as np
from time import time
import torchvision.utils as vutils
from torch.utils.data import Dataset
from torch.utils.data import DataLoader
import matplotlib.pyplot as plt
%matplotlib inline
```

2. Then, implement `Controller`. As part of the controller, we will be implementing the following three components:

- A two-layer feedforward network
- Weight initialization using the Xavier approach
- Sigmoid nonlinearity

```
class Controller(nn.Module):
    def __init__(self, input_size, output_size, hidden_size):
        super(Controller, self).__init__()
        self.layer1 = nn.Linear(input_size, hidden_size)
        self.layer2 = nn.Linear(hidden_size, output_size)
        self.intialize_parameters()

    def intialize_parameters(self):
        # Initialize the weights of linear layers
        nn.init.xavier_uniform_(self.layer1.weight, gain=1.4)
        nn.init.normal_(self.layer1.bias, std=0.01)
        nn.init.xavier_uniform_(self.layer2.weight, gain=1.4)
        nn.init.normal_(self.layer2.bias, std=0.01)

    def forward(self, x, last_read):
        # Forward pass operation, depending on last_read operation
        x = torch.cat((x, last_read), dim=1)
        x = torch.sigmoid(self.layer1(x))
        x = torch.sigmoid(self.layer2(x))
        return x
```

We can have an LSTM controller as well, but because of simplicity, we build a two-layer fully connected controller.

3. Next, implement the `Memory` module. `Memory` is a two-dimensional matrix, with M rows, and N columns:

$$cosine[k_t, M_t] = \frac{k_t \cdot M_t}{|k_t| \cdot |M_t|} \quad ---(CB1)$$

$$w_t^c = \beta_t cosine[k_t, M_t(i)] \quad ---(CB2)$$

$$w_t^c = \frac{\exp(\beta_t cosine[k_t, M_t(i)])}{\sum_j \exp(\beta_t cosine[k_t, M_t(j)])} \quad ---(CB3)$$

$$w_t^g \leftarrow g_t w_t^c + (1 - g_t) w_{t-1} \quad ---(CS1)$$

$$w_t^g = [w_{i-1}^g, w_i^g, w_{i+1}^g] \quad ---(CS2)$$

$$w_t^* \leftarrow \sum_{j=0}^{N-1} w_t^g(j) s_t(i - j) \quad ---(CS3)$$

$$w_t(i) \leftarrow \frac{w_t^*(i)^{\gamma_t}}{\sum_j w_t^*(j)^{\gamma_t}} \quad ---(S1)$$

The `address()` function performs the memory addressing, which is composed of four functions:

- `similarity`
- `interpolate`
- `shift`
- `sharpen`

```
class Memory(nn.Module):
    def __init__(self, M, N, controller_out):
        super(Memory, self).__init__()
        self.N = N
        self.M = M
        self.read_lengths = self.N + 1 + 1 + 3 + 1
        self.write_lengths = self.N + 1 + 1 + 3 + 1 + self.N +
            self.N
        self.w_last = [] # define to keep track of weight_vector
        at each time step.
        self.reset_memory()

    def address(self, k, beta, g, s, gamma, memory, w_last):
        # Content focus
        wc = self._similarity(k, beta, memory) # CB1 to CB3
```

```
    equations
    # Location focus
    wg = self._interpolate(wc, g, w_last) # CS1 equation
    w_hat = self._shift(wg, s) # CS2 and CS3 equation
    w = self._sharpen(w_hat, gamma) # S1 equation
    return w
# Implementing Similarity on basis of CB1 followed by CB2
and CB3 Equation
def _similarity(self, k, beta, memory):
    w = F.cosine_similarity(memory, k, -1, 1e-16) # CB1
    Equation
    w = F.softmax(beta * w, dim=-1) # CB2 and CB3 Equation
    return w # return CB3 equation obtained weights
# Implementing CS1 Equation. It decides whether to use
the weights we obtained
# at the previous time step w_last or use the weight
obtained through similarity(content focus)
def _interpolate(self, wc, g, w_last):
    return g * wc + (1 - g) * w_last
# .... Rest Code is available at Github......
```

4. Next, implement the `read` operation. Here, we will define `ReadHead`, which can access and update memory according to the `read` operations:

$$\sum_i w_t(i) = 1, 0 \le w_t(i) \le 1 \quad --- (R1)$$

$$r_t \leftarrow \sum_i w_t(i) M_t(i) \quad --- (R2)$$

$$M_t^*(i) \leftarrow (1 - w(i)e) M_{t-1}(i) \quad --- (E1)$$

$$M_t(i) \leftarrow M_t^*(i) + w_t(i)\alpha_t \quad --- (A1)$$

```
class ReadHead(Memory):
    # Reading based on R2 equation
    def read(self, memory, w):
        return torch.matmul(w, memory)
    # Use Memory class we formed above to create a ReadHead
    operation
    def forward(self, x, memory):
        param = self.fc_read(x) # gather parameters
        # initialize necessary parameters k, beta, g, shift,
        and gamma
        k, beta, g, s, gamma = torch.split(param,
            [self.N, 1, 1, 3, 1], dim=1)
        k = torch.tanh(k)
        beta = F.softplus(beta)
        g = torch.sigmoid(g)
        s = F.softmax(s, dim=1)
        gamma = 1 + F.softplus(gamma)
```

```
# obtain current weight address vectors from Memory
w = self.address(k, beta, g, s, gamma, memory,
    self.w_last[-1])
# append in w_last function
self.w_last.append(w)
mem = self.read(memory, w)
return mem, w
```

5. Similar to the `read` operation, here we will implement the `write` operation:

```
class WriteHead(Memory):
    def write(self, memory, w, e, a):
        # Implement write function based on E1 and A1 Equation
        w, e, a = torch.squeeze(w), torch.squeeze(e),
            torch.squeeze(a)
        erase = torch.ger(w, e)
        m_tilde = memory * (1 - erase) # E1 equation
        add = torch.ger(w, a)
        memory_update = m_tilde + add # A1 equation
        return memory_update

    def forward(self, x, memory):
        param = self.fc_write(x) # gather parameters
        # initialize necessary parameters k, beta, g, shift,
        and gamma
        k, beta, g, s, gamma, a, e = torch.split(param,
            [self.N, 1, 1, 3, 1, self.N, self.N], dim=1)
        k = torch.tanh(k)
        beta = F.softplus(beta)
        g = torch.sigmoid(g)
        s = F.softmax(s, dim=-1)
        gamma = 1 + F.softplus(gamma)
        a = torch.tanh(a)
        e = torch.sigmoid(e)
        # obtain current weight address vectors from Memory
        w = self.address(k, beta, g, s, gamma, memory,
            self.w_last[-1])
        # append in w_last function
        self.w_last.append(w)
        # obtain current mem location based on R2 equation
        mem = self.write(memory, w, e, a)
        return mem, w
```

Both `ReadHead` and `WriteHead` use a fully connected layer to produce parameters (`k`, `beta`, `g`, `s`, `gamma`) for content addressing.

6. Implement a neural Turing machine structure, which includes the following:

- A fully connected controller
- Read and write heads
- Memory parameters
- Utility functions to operate on memory that is not trainable

```
class NTM(nn.Module):
    def forward(self, X=None):
        if X is None:
            X = torch.zeros(1, self.num_inputs)
        controller_out = self.controller(X, self.last_read)
        self._read_write(controller_out)
        # use updated last_read to get sequence
        out = torch.cat((X, self.last_read), -1)
        out = torch.sigmoid(self.fc_out(out))

        return out

    def _read_write(self, controller_out):
        # Read Operation
        read, w = self.read_head(controller_out, self.memory)
        self.last_read = read
        # Write Operation
        mem, w = self.write_head(controller_out, self.memory)
        self.memory = mem
```

In the `forward` function, X can be `None`. This is because, in a copy task, training happens in two steps for one particular sequence:

1. In the first step, the network is shown k-dimensional input for t time steps.
2. In the second step (the prediction step), the network takes in a k-dimensional zeros vector to produce predictions that perform the copying of the input for each time step.

7. Here, we are generating a random sequence of vectors for the copy task. It is to be copied by the NTM model:

```
class BinaySeqDataset(Dataset):

    def __init__(self, sequence_length, token_size,
    training_samples):
        self.seq_len = sequence_length
        self.seq_width = token_size
```

```
                    self.dataset_dim = training_samples

        def _generate_seq(self):
            # A special token is appened at beginning and end of each
            # sequence which marks sequence boundaries.
            seq = np.random.binomial(1, 0.5, (self.seq_len,
self.seq_width))
            seq = torch.from_numpy(seq)
            # Add start and end token
            inp = torch.zeros(self.seq_len + 2, self.seq_width)
            inp[1:self.seq_len + 1, :self.seq_width] = seq.clone()
            inp[0, 0] = 1.0
            inp[self.seq_len + 1, self.seq_width - 1] = 1.0
            outp = seq.data.clone()

            return inp.float(), outp.float()

        def __len__(self):
            return self.dataset_dim

        def __getitem__(self, idx):
            inp, out = self._generate_seq()
            return inp, out
```

8. We will also implement gradient clipping, as it's generally a good idea to clip gradients so that the network is numerically stable:

```
def clip_grads(net, min_grad=-10,max_grad=10):
    parameters = list(filter(lambda p: p.grad is not None,
net.parameters()))
    for p in parameters:
        p.grad.data.clamp_(min_grad,max_grad)
```

9. Initialize the parameters for training:

```
memory_capacity=64
memory_vector_size=128
controller_output_dim=256
controller_hidden_dim=512
learning_rate=1e-2

sequence_length, token_size, training_samples = 2, 10, 99
min_grad, max_grad = -10, 10
```

10. Then, initialize the train model:

```
# Initialize the dataset
dataset = BinaySeqDataset(sequence_length, token_size,
training_samples)
dataloader = DataLoader(dataset, batch_size=1,shuffle=True,
num_workers=4)
model = NTM() # Initialize NTM
criterion = torch.nn.BCELoss()
optimizer = torch.optim.RMSprop(model.parameters(),
lr=learning_rate)
losses = []
# Train the Model
for e, (X, Y) in enumerate(dataloader):
    tmp = time()
    model.initalize_state()
    optimizer.zero_grad()
    inp_seq_len = sequence_length + 2
    out_seq_len = sequence_length
    X.requires_grad = True
    # Forward Pass: Feed the Sequence
    for t in range(0, inp_seq_len):
        model(X[:, t])
    # Predictions: Obtain the already feeded sequence
    y_pred = torch.zeros(Y.size())
    for i in range(0, out_seq_len):
        y_pred[:, i] = model() # Here, X is passed as None
    loss = criterion(y_pred, Y)
    loss.backward()
    clip_grads(model)
    optimizer.step()
    losses += [loss.item()]
    if (e%10==0):
        print("iteration: {}, Loss:{} ".format(e, loss.item()))
    if e == 5000:
        break
```

After running this cell, you will see the following output:

```
iteration: 0, Loss:0.7466866970062256
iteration: 10, Loss:0.7099956274032593
iteration: 20, Loss:0.6183871626853943
iteration: 30, Loss:0.6750341653823853
iteration: 40, Loss:0.7050653696060181
iteration: 50, Loss:0.7188648581504822
```

11. Define a `plot_signal` function and plot the training loss, `losses`:

```
def plot_signal(grid_image, fig_size=(500,100)):
    plt.figure(figsize=fig_size)
    plt.imshow(grid_image.data.permute(2, 1, 0))

plt.plot(losses)
plt.show()
```

12. Test the NTM model's copy task:

```
X, Y = dataset._generate_seq()
X, Y = X.unsqueeze(0), Y.unsqueeze(0)# Add the batch dimension

model.initalize_state()

for t in range(0, inp_seq_len):
    model(X[:, t])

y_pred = torch.zeros(Y.size())
for i in range(0, out_seq_len):
    y_pred[:, i] = model()

grid_img_truth = vutils.make_grid(Y, normalize=True,
scale_each=True)
grid_img_pred = vutils.make_grid(y_pred, normalize=True,
scale_each=True)

plt.figure(figsize=(200,200))
plt.imshow(grid_img_truth.data.permute(2, 1, 0))

plt.figure(figsize=(200,200))
plt.imshow(grid_img_pred.data.permute(2, 1, 0))
```

Running the preceding code will give the following output:

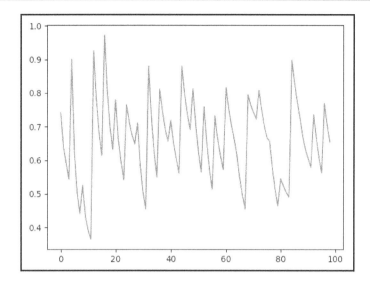

Here, we created a random signal of 300 time steps and saw how well the model copies this signal. In this step, you observed the copy task output. These two signals should be very close; if they aren't, we suggest you train the model more.

Implementation of MAAN

As we showcased in the preceding section, an NTM's controller is capable of using content-based addressing, location-based addressing, or both, whereas MANN works by using a pure content-based memory writer.

MANN also uses a new addressing schema called **least recently used access**. The idea behind this schema is that the least recently used memory location is determined by the read operation and the read operation is performed by content-based addressing. So we basically perform content-based addressing for reading and write to the location that was least recently used.

In this tutorial, we will implement `read` and `write` operations.

1. Let's first import all the libraries that we need:

```
import torch
from torch import nn
import torch.nn.functional as F
import numpy as np
import copy
```

2. Implement the `Memory` module similar to an NTM, with some changes made to the MANN:

```
class Memory(nn.Module):

    def __init__(self, M, N, controller_out):
        super(Memory, self).__init__()
        self.N = N
        self.M = M
        self.read_lengths = self.N + 1 + 1 + 3 + 1
        self.write_lengths = self.N + 1 + 1 + 3 + 1 + self.N + self.N
        self.w_last = [] # define to keep track of weight_vector at
        each time step
        self.reset_memory()

    def address(self, k, beta, g, s, gamma, memory, w_last):
        # Content focus
        w_r = self._similarity(k, beta, memory)
        return w_r

    # Implementing Similarity
    def _similarity(self, k, beta, memory):
        w = F.cosine_similarity(memory, k, -1, 1e-16)
        w = F.softmax(w, dim=-1)
        return w # return w_r^t for reading purpose
```

3. Define `ReadHead` so that it can access and update memory according to `read` operations:

$$cosine[k_t, M_t] = \frac{k_t \cdot M_t}{|k_t| \cdot |M_t|}$$

$$w_t^r = cosine[k_t, M_t(i)]$$

$$w_t^r = \frac{exp(cosine[k_t, M_t(i)])}{\sum exp(cosine[k_t, M_t(j)])}$$

$$r_t \leftarrow \sum_i^R w_t^r(i) M_t(i)$$

The `ReadHead` function is defined as follows:

```
class ReadHead(Memory):
    def read(self, memory, w):
        # Calculate Memory Update
        return torch.matmul(w, memory)

    def forward(self, x, memory):
        param = self.fc_read(x) # gather parameters
        # initialize necessary parameters k, beta, g, shift, and
        gamma
        k, g, s, gamma = torch.split(param, [self.N, 1, 1, 3, 1],
            dim=1)
        k = torch.tanh(k)
        g = F.sigmoid(g)
        s = F.softmax(s, dim=1)
        gamma = 1 + F.softplus(gamma)
        # obtain current weight address vectors from Memory
        w_r = self.address(k, g, s, gamma, memory, self.w_last[-1])
        # append in w_last function to keep track content based
        locations
        self.w_last.append(w_r)
        # obtain current mem location based on above equations
        mem = self.read(memory, w_r)
        w_read = copy.deepcopy(w_r)
        return mem, w_r
```

4. Similar to the `read` operation, here we will implement the `write` operation:

$$w_t^u \leftarrow w_t^r + w_t^w \quad - - - (F1)$$
$$w_t^u \leftarrow \gamma w_{t-1}^u + w_t^r + w_t^w \quad - - - (F2)$$
$$w_t^w \leftarrow \sigma(\alpha)w_{t-1}^r + (1 - \sigma(\alpha))w_{t-1}^{lu} \quad - - - (F3)$$
$$M_t(i) \leftarrow M_{t-1}^i + w_t^w(i)k_t \quad - - - (F4)$$

The `write` operation is implemented as follows:

```
class WriteHead(Memory):

    def usage_weight_vector(self, prev_w_u, w_read, w_write,
    gamma):
        w_u = gamma * prev_w_u + torch.sum(w_read, dim=1) +
            torch.sum(w_write, dim=1)
        return w_u # Equation F2
    def least_used(self, w_u, memory_size=3, n_reads=4):
        _, indices = torch.topk(-1*w_u, k=n_reads)
        wlu_t = torch.sum(F.one_hot(indices,
            memory_size).type(torch.FloatTensor),dim=1,
```

```
                keepdim=True)
        return indices, wlu_t
    def mann_write(self, memory, w_write, a, gamma, prev_w_u,
    w_read, k):
        w_u = self.usage_weight_vector(prev_w_u, w_read, w_write,
            gamma)
        w_least_used_weight_t = self.least_used(w_u)
        # Implement write step as per (F3) Equation
        w_write = torch.sigmoid(a)*w_read +
            (1-torch.sigmoid(a))*w_least_used_weight_t
        memory_update = memory + w_write*k # Memory Update
        as per Equation (F4)
    def forward(self, x, memory):
        param = self.fc_write(x) # gather parameters
        k, beta, g, s, gamma, a, e = torch.split(param,
            [self.N, 1, 1, 3, 1, self.N, self.N], dim=1)
        k = F.tanh(k)
        beta = F.softplus(beta)
        g = F.sigmoid(g)
        s = F.softmax(s, dim=-1)
        gamma = 1 + F.softplus(gamma)
        a = F.tanh(a)
        # obtain current weight address vectors from Memory
        w_write = self.address(k, beta, g, s, gamma, memory,
            self.w_last[-1])
        # append in w_last function to keep track content
        based locations
        self.w_last.append(w_write)
        # obtain current mem location based on F2-F4 equations
        mem = self.write(memory, w_write, a, gamma, prev_w_u,
            w_read, k)
        w_write = copy.deepcopy(w)
        return mem, w
```

Both `ReadHead` and `WriteHead` use a fully connected layer to produce parameters (`k`, `beta`, `g`, `s`, and `gamma`) for content addressing.

 Note that, this exercise is just to showcase how MANN is inspired by NTM. If you wish to explore the preceding exercise on a real-world dataset, please refer to the GitHub repository at `https://github.com/PacktPublishing/Hands-On-One-shot-Learning-with-Python/tree/master/Chapter03`.

Summary

In this chapter, we explored different forms of model-based architectures for one-shot learning. The most common thing we observed is the use of external memory, and how this can be helpful in learning representations at different stages of a neural network. NMT methods perform well on one-shot learning tasks, but they still have limited capacity because of hand-engineered memory-addressing functions, as they have to be differentiable. It might be interesting to explore more complex functions to address the memory. In meta networks, we saw how one new network was defined to enable fast learning of the original network, and how storing information about representations at the meta-learner level was useful to fine-tune parameters at the base level. Although model-based architectures are a good method of implementing one-shot learning, they come with the prerequisite of external memory, and so the cost of implementing a model-based architecture is expensive compared to other methods.

In the next chapter, we will go through optimization-based methods, such as model-agnostic meta-learning and LSTM meta-learning. As memory gives us a way to store the information that we have learned, the optimization strategy gives us the ability to learn things faster. We will explore some different forms of optimization strategies that can be implemented to learn the objective in a few examples in later chapters.

Questions

1. What are neural Turing machines, and how do they help in learning?
2. How does the memory matrix help the model to learn faster?
3. How does fragmentation among the meta-learner and the base learner help the architecture to learn one-shot learning?

Further reading

Model-based methods are one of the more complicated topics that you will need to learn about, so if you wish to dig deeper into the concepts involved, you can read through the following papers:

- *Neural Turing Machines*: https://arxiv.org/pdf/1410.5401.pdf
- *Memory-augmented neural networks*: http://proceedings.mlr.press/v48/santoro16.pdf
- *Meta networks*: https://arxiv.org/pdf/1703.00837.pdf

Optimization-Based Methods

4

Most deep learning models learn objectives using the gradient-descent method; however, gradient-descent optimization requires a large number of training samples for a model to converge, which makes it unfit for few-shot learning. In generic deep learning models, we train our models to learn to accomplish a definite objective, whereas humans train to learn any objective. Following this observation, various researchers have created different optimization approaches that focus on **learn-to-learn** mechanisms.

In other words, the system focuses on how to converge any loss function (objective) instead of minimizing a single loss function (objective), which makes this algorithmic approach task and domain invariant. For example, you don't need to train a model to recognize types of flowers using a cross-entropy loss function; instead, you can train the model to learn to understand the difference between any two images, which in turn will make the model task agnostic (for example, flower recognition, flower detection) and domain agnostic (for example, cat recognition).

In this chapter, we will cover the following topics:

- Overview of gradient descent
- Understanding model-agnostic meta-learning
- Understanding LSTM meta-learner
- Coding exercises

Technical requirements

The Python, Anaconda, Jupyter Notebook, Matplotlib, and Scikit-learn libraries will be required to learn and execute the project in this chapter.

You can find the code files for this chapter from the GitHub repository of this book at `https://github.com/PacktPublishing/Hands-On-One-shot-Learning-with-Python`.

Overview of gradient descent

If we look into the learning method of neural network architectures, it usually consists of a lot of parameters and is optimized using a gradient-descent algorithm, which takes many iterative steps over many examples to perform well. The gradient descent algorithm, however, provides a decent performance in its models, but there are scenarios where the gradient-descent optimization algorithm fails. Let's look at such scenarios in the coming sections.

There are mainly two reasons why the gradient-descent algorithm fails to optimize a neural network when a limited amount of data is given:

- For each new task, the neural network has to start from a random initialization of its parameters, which results in late convergence. Transfer learning has been used to alleviate this problem by using a pretrained network, but it is constrained in that the data should be of a similar domain.
- Even variants of gradient descent's weight-updating step methods (such as AdaGrad, Adam, RMS, and so on) can't perform well with a lower number of epochs. These algorithms can't guarantee convergence, especially when used for nonconvex optimization.

What can be really helpful is to learn some common initializations that can be used across all domains as a good point of initialization. The key idea of a gradient-descent algorithm is based on the direction of the next step, which is chosen on the basis of a probabilistic distribution assumption. So, if we are somehow able to approximate that probabilistic distribution completely, we will be able to optimize the network with only a few steps. This is the basic idea of optimization-based algorithms for one-/few-shot learning.

Understanding model-agnostic meta-learning

Model-agnostic meta-learning (**MAML**) attempts to solve the shortcomings of the gradient-descent approach by providing better weight initialization for every new task. The key idea of this approach is to train the models' parameters using a different dataset. When using it for a new task, the model gives better performance by using already initialized parameters to fine-tune the architecture through one or more gradient steps. This method of training a model's parameters so that a few gradient steps can optimize the loss function can also be viewed, from a feature-learning standpoint, as building an internal representation. In this approach, we choose a generic model's architecture so that it can be used for various tasks. The primary contribution of MAML is a simple model- and task-agnostic fast learning algorithm.

Understanding the logic behind MAML

The objective of MAML is to provide a good initialization of a model's parameters in order to achieve optimal fast learning on a new task with fewer gradient steps. It also attempts to avoid overfitting scenarios, which happens while training a neural network with less data architecture. The following diagram is a representation of MAML:

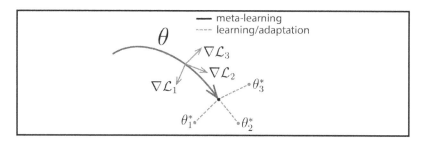

As we can see in the preceding diagram, θ is the model's parameter and the bold black line is the meta-learning phase. Let's assume that we have three different new tasks and a gradient step is taken for each task (the gray lines with the arrowheads). We can see that the parameters, θ, are close to all three optimal parameters of the three tasks, which makes θ the best parameter initialization that can quickly adapt to different new tasks. As a result, only a small change in the parameters, θ, will lead to an optimal minimization of the loss function of any task. Following this observation, MAML suggests that we should first learn θ through the primary dataset; while fine-tuning on the real dataset, we just move a small step.

As the name suggests, model-agnostic meta-learning can be used for any form of a model, be it classification, regression, or reinforcement learning. But for this book, we will just focus on the one-shot learning classification aspect of the MAML algorithm. So, let's begin!

Algorithm

To learn about the one-/few-shot learning aspects of MAML, first, we need to learn certain terms. These are similar to what we learned when matching networks:

- **T**: This represents various tasks—for example, we want our model to learn to identify cats, dogs, horses, and so on, and T_i represents a training model to identify cats, for example. Here, $T_i \in T$.
- **P(T)**: This represents the probabilistic distribution across all tasks. Our aim is to learn *P(T)* through MAML.
- **L(T)**: This represents the loss function generated by task, *T*, data points. For classification, we can use cross-entropy loss:

$$L(f(x), y) = \sum_{x,y->T} y * log(f(x)) + (1 - y) * log(1 - f(x))$$

Suppose we wish to train a classification model, f_θ, that can learn to recognize cats, dogs, and horses in an image. Let's go through a step-by-step process of how to set up the MAML:

1. Randomly initialize model parameters—$\theta \sim N(0, 1)$.
2. Repeat until this is done.
3. Sample *Ti* from *P(T)*—for example, we randomly sample the task of recognizing cats from all possible tasks.

4. For all T_i sampled from *P(T)*, do the following:

- Sample K training data points, $D_i = (x_i, y_i)$, from T_i (K = 1, for one-shot learning).
- Forward-pass through layers(f_θ) to calculate L_{T_i} and $\nabla_\theta L_{T_i} f_\theta$.
- Update parameters using the gradient-descent method. Since we are training our model for a particular task, we will learn θ'_i (task-specific parameters):

$$\theta'_i = \theta - \alpha \nabla_\theta L_{T_i} (f_\theta)$$

- Sample test data points, $D'_i = (x_i, y_i)$, from T_i for a meta update.

End the `for` loop.

5. Update θ by calculating the loss and its gradient using sampled test data points, D'_i, on model $f_{\theta'_i}$:

$$\theta \leftarrow \theta - \beta \nabla_\theta \sum_{T_i \sim P(T)} L_{T_i} (f_{\theta'_i})$$

End the `repeat` loop.

MAML has been able to achieve better performance than Siamese networks, matching networks, and memory-augmented neural networks for the Omniglot and mini-ImageNet datasets. As MAML is proven to be a better performer, there are various other tasks where MAML can be used. Let's go through one such variant—**domain-adaptive meta-learning (DAML)**.

MAML application – domain-adaptive meta-learning

When it comes to imitation learning, robots need to receive proper data consisting of information about kinesthetic changes (awareness about their body parts movements), teleoperation (control), and other kinds of input. On the other hand, a human brain can learn simply by watching some videos. DAML attempted to solve the problem of imitation learning by using meta-learning (MAML). It proposed a system for learning robotic manipulation skills from a single video of human, by just leveraging strong priors (for example, information on kinesthetic learning) extracted through data from different tasks, as shown in the following diagram:

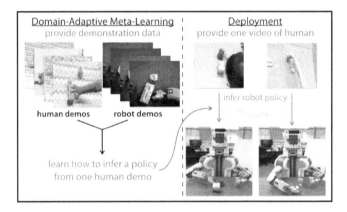

As robots can't be trained using imitation-learning loss functions, DAML proposed a behavior-cloning objective, **temporal loss**, which also acts as a regularization term in log space. As we know, having strong regularization is important in any scenario to avoid overfitting, especially in the case of one-shot learning.

Understanding LSTM meta-learner

The LSTM meta-learner is a type of meta-learning. The LSTM meta-learner has two phases:

- **Meta-learner**: In this phase, the model focuses on learning general knowledge across various tasks.
- **Base learner**: In the base learner, the model tries to optimize to learn parameters for a task-specific objective.

The key idea of the LSTM meta-learner is to train an LSTM cell to *learn an update rule* for our original task. In meta-learning framework terms, an **LSTM cell** will be used as the meta-learner, whereas *task-specific objectives*, such as dog breed classification, will be the *base learner*.

Now, the question arises, why would we use an LSTM cell? The authors of the LSTM meta-learner made a key observation that a cell-state update in LSTM is similar to a gradient-based update in backpropagation, and can be used to learn the update rule of the base learner objective:

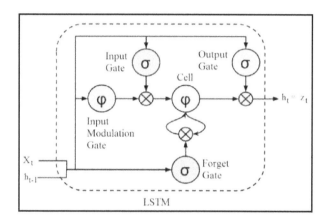

LSTMs store information history with the help of various gates, as shown in the preceding diagram. We are also aware that there are various variations of **stochastic gradient descent** (**SGD**), such as momentum, RMSprop, Adam, and many more, which essentially store information about past learning (in the form of gradients) to enable better optimization. Therefore, logically, an LSTM cell can be thought of as a better optimizing strategy that enables the model to capture the knowledge of both the short term of a particular task and the common long term.

In the next section, we will gain an understanding of the architecture, the logic behind the LSTM cell, and the weight update algorithm.

Architecture of the LSTM meta-learner

If we look into the update method of gradient descent, we will see an equation like this:

$$\theta_t = \theta_{t-1} - \alpha_t \nabla L_t$$

Here, θ_t is the parameter at time step t, ∇L_t is the gradient of loss at t, and α_t is the learning rate at time t.

A cell update equation of an LSTM cell, on the other hand, looks something like this:

$$c_t = f_t \odot c_{t-1} + i_t \odot \bar{c_t}$$

This update looks very similar to how cells get updated in LSTMs. The authors of LSTM meta-learner proposed that if we put the following values in the cell-update equation, then we will get a gradient descent update rule:

$$f_t = 1$$
$$c_{t-1} = \theta_{t-1}$$
$$i_t = \alpha_t$$
$$\bar{c_t} = \nabla L_t$$

Considering this, logically, we just want to learn i_t, as that is essentially similar to estimating the *learning rate* of the gradient descent. So, LSTM meta-learner defines i_t as the following:

$$i_t = \sigma(W_I . [\nabla L_t, L_t, \theta_{t-1}, i_{t-1}] + b_I)$$

Essentially, i_t is defined as a sigmoid function with a combination of the current gradient, current loss, and previous learning rate, i_{t-1}.

For f_t, it should be 1, but to avoid problems of shrinking gradients, it was defined as follows:

$$f_t = \sigma(W_F . [\nabla L_t, L_t, \theta_{t-1}, f_{t-1}] + b_F)$$

Essentially, f_t is defined as a sigmoid function with a combination of the current gradient, current loss, and forget gate.

You might wonder why they used this particular choice of LSTM cell? If we look closely, both i_t and f_t have been chosen as a function of the current gradient and current loss. This has been done intentionally to enable the meta-learner to *control the learning rate* so as to train the base learner in less time.

Data preprocessing

In a general deep learning setting, to train a model on a given dataset, *D*, we divide our dataset into three parts—training, validation, and test set. But in the meta-learning setting, we first divide the dataset into task-specific sets (for example, cat breed classification and dog breed classification) known as **meta sets**, say D_n. For each $D \epsilon D_n$ consists of $D_{n-train}$ and D_{n-test}, so for *K*-shot learning, each $D_{n-train}$ consists of *K*N* examples, where *N* is the number of classes.

After this, $D_{n-train}$ is further divided into three parts: $D_{meta-train}$, $D_{meta-validation}$, and $D_{meta-test}$. Here, the objective is to use $D_{meta-train}$ for training a *learning algorithm* that can take any task-specific sets as training sets D_{train} and produce a better classifier (learner).

Algorithm – pseudocode implementation

To train a one-shot learning model, you need to match training conditions to test time conditions—for example, training on less data but across several batches, just as we did in matching networks. LSTM meta-learner also follows the same concept as matching networks and has been proven to perform really well at task-specific objectives.

To begin understanding the LSTM meta-learner, first, we need to understand certain terms:

- **Base learner** (**M**): Main task-specific objective, with parameters, θ—for example, a classifier to detect cats
- **Meta-learner** (**R**): LSTM cell, with parameters, $\ominus$
- **Data points** (**X, Y**): Data points sampled from $D_{meta-train}$
- **Loss** (**L**): Loss function used to tune the main task-specific objective—for example, binary cross-entropy loss

Let's begin going through the LSTM meta-learner algorithm step by step:

1. First, randomly initialize the initial parameters ($\ominus_0$) of the LSTM cell.
2. For D = 1 to n steps, do the following:

   - Randomly sample D_{train}, D_{test} from $D_{meta-train}$.
   - Randomly initialize the initial parameters (θ_0) of the base learner (classification model).
   - For t = 1 to T steps, repeat the following:
     - Randomly sample the input-output pairs (X_t, Y_t) from D_{train}.
     - Calculate the loss of the base learner (classification model) using $L_t = L(M(X_t; \theta_{t-1}), Y_t)$.
     - Update the cell state (c_t) using the loss (L_t) and its gradient ($\nabla_{\theta_{t-1}} L_t$) of the base learner using the cell-state equation.
     - Update the base learner (classification model) parameters as $\theta_t = c_t$ (refer to the *Architecture of the LSTM meta-learner* section).

   End the T-steps loop.

   - Now, randomly sample the input-output pairs (X_{test}, Y_{test}) from D_{test}.
   - Calculate the loss of the base learner (classification model) using $L_{test} = L(M(X_{test}; \theta_T), Y_{test})$.
   - Update the meta-learner (LSTM cell) parameters ($\ominus_t$) using $\nabla_{\ominus_{d-1}} L_{test}$ (refer to the *Architecture of LSTM meta-learner* section).

   End the n-steps loop.

In short, while iterating through T steps, the base-learner parameters get updated. After T-steps, the final base-learner parameters are then used to evaluate the test set and make updates on the meta-learner parameters. For a pictorial representation of the algorithm, refer to the following diagram of the architecture:

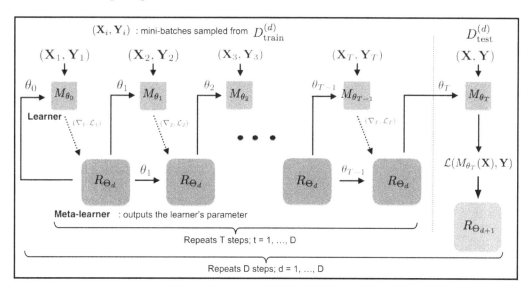

The overall idea of LSTM meta-learner looks very compelling. You might wonder why we use only one LSTM cell, and why the authors of LSTM meta-learner didn't use the whole LSTM network just as we saw in matching networks. It's true that you can add some complex architecture to a meta-learner, but it comes at the cost of a large number of parameters to train. The use of the LSTM cell has made this meta-learning architecture feasible for one-shot learning.

In the next section, we will go through coding exercises for MAML and LSTM meta-learner, which will help us understand the architectures more thoroughly.

Exercises

In this section, we will first go through a simple exercise of regression of sinusoidal data using MAML.

A simple implementation of model-agnostic meta-learning

For this tutorial, we will be showcasing how we can apply MAML to learn a simple curve of sinusoidal data. The second part of this tutorial is available on GitHub, where we can learn about how to train MAML on mini-ImageNet using the torch-meta library.

Let's begin this tutorial by going through the following steps:

1. Import all libraries:

    ```
    import math
    import random
    import torch
    from torch import nn
    from torch.nn import functional as F
    import matplotlib as mpl
    mpl.use('Agg')
    import matplotlib.pyplot as plt
    %matplotlib inline
    ```

2. Create a simple neural network architecture. We will be getting randomly generated data of the sinusoidal curve. We will be using this very small network, as we don't need a big one to learn a curve:

    ```
    def net(x, params):
        x = F.linear(x, params[0], params[1])
        x = F.relu(x)

        x = F.linear(x, params[2], params[3])
        x = F.relu(x)

        x = F.linear(x, params[4], params[5])
        return x

    params = [
        torch.Tensor(32, 1).uniform_(-1., 1.).requires_grad_(),
        torch.Tensor(32).zero_().requires_grad_(),

        torch.Tensor(32, 32).uniform_(-1./math.sqrt(32),
            1./math.sqrt(32)).requires_grad_(),
        torch.Tensor(32).zero_().requires_grad_(),

        torch.Tensor(1, 32).uniform_(-1./math.sqrt(32),
            1./math.sqrt(32)).requires_grad_(),
    ```

```
        torch.Tensor(1).zero_().requires_grad_(),
]
```

3. Set up the parameters for training. Initialize the parameters for the alpha, beta, learning rate, optimizer, and number of loops:

```
opt = torch.optim.SGD(params, lr=1e-2)
n_inner_loop = 5
alpha = 3e-2
```

4. Implement the optimization algorithm:

```
for it in range(100000): # training for large number of iterations
    b = 0 if random.choice([True, False]) else math.pi # setting up
            beta variable randomly
    #### Randomly obtain task 1 sinusoidal data ####
    x = torch.rand(4, 1)*4*math.pi - 2*math.pi
    y = torch.sin(x + b)
    #### Randomly obtain the task 2 sinusoidal data ####
    v_x = torch.rand(4, 1)*4*math.pi - 2*math.pi
    v_y = torch.sin(v_x + b)
    opt.zero_grad() # setup optimizer
    new_params = params # initialize weights for inner loop
    for k in range(n_inner_loop):
        f = net(x, new_params) # re-initialize task 2 neural
            network with new parameters
        loss = F.l1_loss(f, y) # set loss as L1 Loss
        grads = torch.autograd.grad(loss, new_params,
            create_graph=True)
        new_params = [(new_params[i] - alpha*grads[i]) for i in
            range(len(params))] # update weights of inner loop
    v_f = net(v_x, new_params) # re-initialize task 1 neural
        network with new parameters
    loss2 = F.l1_loss(v_f, v_y) # calculate Loss
    loss2.backward() # Backward Pass
    opt.step()
```

After running this, you will see the optimization output in the following form:

```
Iteration 0 -- Inner loop 0 -- Loss: 0.3558
Iteration 0 -- Inner loop 1 -- Loss: 0.3815
Iteration 0 -- Inner loop 2 -- Loss: 0.3788
Iteration 0 -- Inner loop 3 -- Loss: 0.3265
Iteration 0 -- Inner loop 4 -- Loss: 0.4066
Iteration 0 -- Outer Loss: 0.7631
Iteration 100 -- Inner loop 0 -- Loss: 0.9611
Iteration 100 -- Inner loop 1 -- Loss: 0.9364
Iteration 100 -- Inner loop 2 -- Loss: 0.9122
```

```
Iteration 100 -- Inner loop 3 -- Loss: 0.8883
Iteration 100 -- Inner loop 4 -- Loss: 0.8641
Iteration 100 -- Outer Loss: 1.0115
```

5. Plot the results that you obtained. Once we have obtained the right parameters, we will first generate some random data points to sub-sample five data points. If we plot the results, we will see that the neural net was able to obtain the correct curve on the sinusoidal data points:

```python
# Randomly generate 5 data points.
t_b = math.pi
t_x = torch.rand(4, 1)*4*math.pi - 2*math.pi
t_y = torch.sin(t_x + t_b)

opt.zero_grad()

t_params = params
for k in range(n_inner_loop):
    t_f = net(t_x, t_params)
    t_loss = F.l1_loss(t_f, t_y)

    grads = torch.autograd.grad(t_loss, t_params,
        create_graph=True)
    t_params = [(t_params[i] - alpha*grads[i]) for i
        in range(len(params))]

test_x = torch.arange(-2*math.pi, 2*math.pi,
step=0.01).unsqueeze(1)
test_y = torch.sin(test_x + t_b)

test_f = net(test_x, t_params)

plt.plot(test_x.data.numpy(), test_y.data.numpy(), label='sin(x)')
plt.plot(test_x.data.numpy(), test_f.data.numpy(), label='net(x)')
plt.plot(t_x.data.numpy(), t_y.data.numpy(), 'o', label='Examples')
plt.legend()
plt.savefig('maml_output.png')
```

After running this, you should be able to obtain a graph like the following:

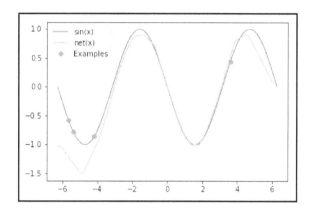

If you look at the graph, you will see that net was able to learn the sin(x) curve approximately.

A simple implementation of domain-adaption meta-learning

For this tutorial, we will be using domain-adaption meta-learning to learn a simple curve of sinusoidal data. It's a variation of model-agnostic meta-learning, but with added prior information—that is, extra relevant information about the domain is already added.

Let's begin!

Meta-learning algorithms optimize the ability of models to learn new tasks quickly. To do so, they use data collected across a wide range of tasks and are evaluated based on their ability to learn new meta-test tasks. This process can be formalized as learning a prior (that is extracting important information) over data (a range of tasks), and the fine-tuning process becomes the inference under the learned prior:

1. Import all of the libraries:

```
import math
import random
import sys
import torch # v0.4.1
from torch import nn
from torch.nn import functional as F
from tqdm import tqdm
```

```
from time import sleep
import matplotlib as mpl
mpl.use('Agg')
import matplotlib.pyplot as plt
%matplotlib inline
import warnings
warnings.filterwarnings('ignore')
```

2. Create a simple neural network architecture that will learn the sinusoidal curve. We will be getting randomly generated data from the sinusoidal curve, so we will be using this very small network, as we won't need a big one to learn a curve:

```
def meta_net(x, params):
    # main network which is suppose to learn our main objective
    i.e; learn sinusoidal curve family here.
    x = F.linear(x, params[0], params[1])
    x1 = F.relu(x)

    x = F.linear(x1, params[2], params[3])
    x2 = F.relu(x)

    y = F.linear(x2, params[4], params[5])

    return y, x2, x1

params = [
    torch.Tensor(32, 1).uniform_(-1., 1.).requires_grad_(),
    torch.Tensor(32).zero_().requires_grad_(),

    torch.Tensor(32, 32).uniform_(-1./math.sqrt(32),
        1./math.sqrt(32)).requires_grad_(),
    torch.Tensor(32).zero_().requires_grad_(),

    torch.Tensor(1, 32).uniform_(-1./math.sqrt(32),
        1./math.sqrt(32)).requires_grad_(),
    torch.Tensor(1).zero_().requires_grad_(),
]
```

3. Create another simple neural network architecture for adding prior information about the domain. We will be adding a piece of prior knowledge to our main net; therefore, we need to create a simple `adap_net`:

```
def adap_net(y, x2, x1, params):
    # the net takes forward pass from meta_net and provides
    efficient parameter initializations.
```

```
    # It works adapts the meta_net easily to any form of change
    x = torch.cat([y, x2, x1], dim=1)

    x = F.linear(x, params[0], params[1])
    x = F.relu(x)

    x = F.linear(x, params[2], params[3])
    x = F.relu(x)

    x = F.linear(x, params[4], params[5])

    return x

adap_params = [
    torch.Tensor(32, 1+32+32).uniform_(-1./math.sqrt(65),
        1./math.sqrt(65)).requires_grad_(),
    torch.Tensor(32).zero_().requires_grad_(),

    torch.Tensor(32, 32).uniform_(-1./math.sqrt(32),
        1./math.sqrt(32)).requires_grad_(),
    torch.Tensor(32).zero_().requires_grad_(),

    torch.Tensor(1, 32).uniform_(-1./math.sqrt(32),
        1./math.sqrt(32)).requires_grad_(),
    torch.Tensor(1).zero_().requires_grad_(),
]
```

4. Set up the parameters for training. We are going to use inner-loop as opposed to outer-loop training, and therefore, we need to set certain parameters, such as the alpha, beta, learning rate, optimizer, and the number of loops:

```
opt = torch.optim.SGD(params + adap_params, lr=1e-2)
n_inner_loop = 5
alpha = 3e-2
```

5. Implement the optimization algorithm. As mentioned in the *Domain-adaptive meta-learning* section, this approach can learn new skills from only one video of a human. To do this, it first trains the meta-network to build a strong and rich prior over tasks during a meta-training phase, using both human demonstrations and teleoperated demonstrations:

```
inner_loop_loss=[]
outer_lopp_loss=[]
# Here, T ~ p(T ) {or minibatch of tasks} is to learn sinusoidal
family curves
with tqdm(total=100000, file=sys.stdout) as pbar:
    for it in range(100000):
```

```
b = 0 if random.choice([True, False]) else math.pi
#### Randomly obtain the task 2 sinusoidal data ####
v_x = torch.rand(4, 1)*4*math.pi - 2*math.pi
v_y = torch.sin(v_x + b)
opt.zero_grad()
new_params = params
for k in range(n_inner_loop):
    sampled_data = torch.FloatTensor([[random.uniform
        (math.pi/4, math.pi/2) if b == 0
        else random.uniform(-math.pi/2, -math.pi/4)]])
    # Here, si is adap_net parameters: adap_params and
    theta is meta_net parameters
    f, f2, f1 = meta_net(sampled_data, new_params)
    h = adap_net(f, f2, f1, adap_params)
    adap_loss = F.l1_loss(h, torch.zeros(1, 1)) # Calculate
    Loss
    grads = torch.autograd.grad(adap_loss, new_params,
        create_graph=True)
    # Compute policy parameters phi_t(new_params)
    new_params = [(new_params[i] - alpha*grads[i]) for i
        in range(len(params))]
    if it % 100 == 0:
        inner_loop_loss.append(adap_loss)
v_f, _, _ = meta_net(v_x, new_params) # forward pass using
learned policy parameters
loss = F.l1_loss(v_f, v_y) # calculate the loss of meta_net
loss.backward()
opt.step() # optimize the policy parameters(theta and si)
pbar.update(1)
if it % 100 == 0:
    outer_lopp_loss.append(loss)
```

In this phase, the robot (`meta_net`) learns how to learn from humans using data. After the meta-training phase, the robot can acquire new skills by combining its learned prior knowledge with one video of a human performing the new skill. This approach consists of two phases:

- In the meta-training phase, the goal will be to acquire a prior policy (*phi*) using both human and robot demonstration data
- Use a learned prior to quickly learn how to imitate new tasks with only a few data points

Once you run the preceding code, you will get the following output:

```
Iteration 0 -- Inner loop 0 -- Loss: 0.0211
Iteration 0 -- Inner loop 1 -- Loss: 0.0183
Iteration 0 -- Inner loop 2 -- Loss: 0.0225
Iteration 0 -- Inner loop 3 -- Loss: 0.0180
Iteration 0 -- Inner loop 4 -- Loss: 0.0156
Iteration 0 -- Outer Loss: 0.5667
Iteration 100 -- Inner loop 0 -- Loss: 0.0009
Iteration 100 -- Inner loop 1 -- Loss: 0.0007
Iteration 100 -- Inner loop 2 -- Loss: 0.0003
Iteration 100 -- Inner loop 3 -- Loss: 0.0003
Iteration 100 -- Inner loop 4 -- Loss: 0.0000
Iteration 100 -- Outer Loss: 0.8096 ...
```

6. Fine-tune the main net. Once we have obtained the right parameters, we will first generate some random data points to subsample five data points and fine-tune the main meta_net using the loss of adap_net:

```
t_b = math.pi
opt.zero_grad()
t_params = params

for k in range(n_inner_loop):
    # sample the new task data
    new_task_data = torch.FloatTensor([[random.uniform
            (math.pi/4, math.pi/2) if t_b == 0
            else random.uniform(-math.pi/2, -math.pi/4)]])
    # forward pass through meta_net to extract the input for
    adap_net
    t_f, t_f2, t_f1 = meta_net(new_task_data, t_params)
    # extract the information from adap_net
    t_h = adap_net(t_f, t_f2, t_f1, adap_params)
    # calculate the loss, here we used true label as
    torch.zeros(1, 1), because t_b = pi
    t_adap_loss = F.l1_loss(t_h, torch.zeros(1, 1))

    grads = torch.autograd.grad(t_adap_loss, t_params,
        create_graph=True)
    # learn the policy using the loss of adap_net
    t_params = [(t_params[i] - alpha*grads[i]) for i
        in range(len(params))]
```

When deployed, the robot can adapt to a particular task with novel objects using just a single video of a human performing the task with those objects.

7. Visualize the outputs using the following code:

```
test_x = torch.arange(-2*math.pi, 2*math.pi,
step=0.01).unsqueeze(1)
test_y = torch.sin(test_x + t_b)

test_f, _, _ = meta_net(test_x, t_params) # use the learned
parameters

plt.plot(test_x.data.numpy(), test_y.data.numpy(), label='sin(x)')
plt.plot(test_x.data.numpy(), test_f.data.numpy(),
label='meta_net(x)')
plt.legend()
plt.savefig('daml-sine.png')
```

After running the code, you will see a graph similar to the following:

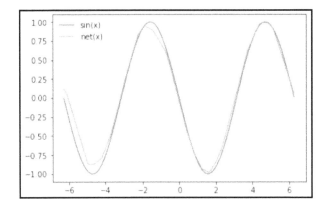

 If you are unable to achieve perfect sine curve shape, double the number of iterations.

Here, you can see that our net model—the orange line—was very close to the real dataset—the blue line. If you wish to explore these models using a real-world dataset, please refer to the GitHub repository at https://github.com/PacktPublishing/Hands-On-One-shot-Learning-with-Python/tree/master/Chapter04. There, you will find other optimization algorithms using the Omniglot and mini-ImageNet datasets.

Summary

To solve any equation, we usually have a lot of methods available to us. Similarly, for optimization (learning the parameters of a neural network), there have been lots of methods that have been open sourced by various researchers, but gradient descent has been proven to be a universal method that can work for every scenario. If we wish to go to a specific type of neural network problem, then it's better to explore different optimization techniques that might be suitable for our task.

In this chapter, we looked at two of the most famous approaches for one-shot learning optimization: MAML and LSTM meta-learner. We learned how MAML approaches the one-shot learning problem by optimizing our initial parameter setting so that one or a few steps of gradient descent on a few data points can lead to better generalization. We also explored the insights given by LSTM meta-learner on how to train an LSTM cell as a meta-learner to predict the weight update of a base learner.

In the next chapter, we will explore one of the well-known ML approaches, Bayesian learning. We will observe the development of a few-shot Bayesian learning framework by representing object categories with probabilistic models. We will go through a proper explanation of discriminative *K*-shot learning and Bayesian program learning, along with their applications in the real world.

Questions

1. What are the pros and cons of the gradient descent optimization algorithm?
2. Are there any alternatives to the gradient descent optimization algorithm?
3. Why are so many epochs needed to train a neural network?

Further reading

For more detail some of the architectures that we looked at in this chapter, I would suggest reading the following papers:

- *Model-agnostic meta-learning*: https://arxiv.org/pdf/1703.03400.pdf
- *Optimization as a model for few-shot learning*: https://openreview.net/pdf?id=rJY0-Kcll

Section 3: Other Methods and Conclusion 3

Deep learning architectures have proven to be highly effective, but they are still not the best approach for one-shot learning. Different Bayesian approaches, such as the Bayesian programming language, can still beat humans at one-shot learning. In this section, we will learn about Bayesian methods and discuss the recent advancements that have been made in this domain. Additionally, we will compare the Bayesian method to a well-known technique—transfer learning—that exists in the deep learning circle to solve any problem. We will also learn when to use the one-shot approach over transfer learning.

This section comprises the following chapters:

- Chapter 5, *Generative Modeling-Based Methods*
- Chapter 6, *Conclusions and Other Approaches*

5
Generative Modeling-Based Methods

When humans make inferences about unseen data, they make use of strong prior knowledge (or inductive bias) about related events they've seen, heard, touched, or experienced. For example, an infant who has grown up with a dog may see a cat for the first time and immediately infer that it shares similarities with the pet-like temperament of the household dog. Of course, cats and dogs as species and individuals are wildly different; however, it's fair to say that a cat is more similar to a dog than other random things the child has experienced—such as food. Humans, as opposed to machine learning models, don't need thousands of examples of cats to *learn* that category from scratch once they have already learned to recognize a dog. The human brain has this innate capability of *learning to learn*, which is related to **transfer learning** and **multi-task learning** in machine learning language. This capability accelerates the learning of new concepts by capitalizing on knowledge learned from related tasks.

Generative models are probabilistic models that aim to bridge the gap between human learning and machine learning. These models aim to learn high-level abstract features from parts of an object and apply those learned features to new but similar object categories. In this chapter, we will study how these generative models are built, what it means to have prior knowledge, how to frame the prior knowledge in mathematical terms, how to learn high-level concepts from a few objects (parameter-learning of the model), and how to combine this newly learned knowledge with prior knowledge to make meaningful decisions about new objects (inference).

The following topics will be covered in this chapter:

- Overview of Bayesian learning
- Understanding directed graphical models
- Overview of probabilistic methods
- Bayesian program learning
- Discriminative k-shot learning

Technical requirements

This chapter will be theory based, so there are no formal technical requirements, but a basic understanding of Bayesian modeling is required.

Overview of Bayesian learning

In this section, we will briefly discuss the idea behind Bayesian learning from a mathematical perspective, which is the core of the probabilistic models for one-shot learning. The overall goal of Bayesian learning is to model the distribution of the parameters, θ, given the training data, that is, to learn the distribution, $P(\theta|Data)$.

In the probabilistic view of machine learning, we try to solve the following equation:

$$P(\theta|Data) = \frac{P(Data|\theta)P(\theta)}{P(Data)}$$

In this setting, we try to find the best set of parameters, theta (θ), that would explain the data. Consequently, we maximize the given equation over θ:

$$argmax_\theta P(\theta|Data) = argmax_\theta \frac{P(Data|\theta)P(\theta)}{P(Dtata)}$$

We can take the logarithm on both sides, which would not affect the optimization problem but makes the math easy and tractable:

$$argmax_\theta \log P(\theta|Data) = argmax_\theta(\log P(Data|\theta) + \log P(\theta) - logP(Data))$$

We can drop the *P(data)* from the right side of the data as it is not dependent on θ for the optimization problem, and consequently, the optimization problem becomes the following:

$$argmax_\theta(\log P(Data|\theta) + \log P(\theta))$$

In a non-probabilistic view (also called the **expectation-maximization framework**), the terms in the equation on the right, $p(Data|\theta)$ and $P(\theta)$, become the loss function and the regularization respectively. The same terms in the given probabilistic setting are called the **likelihood** (of the data, given θ) and the **prior** (prior belief in the parameter space). This probabilistic optimization is called **Maximum A Posterior** (**MAP**) estimation, as we are maximizing the posterior distribution of parameters of the model from the data. However, Bayesian statistics doesn't believe in MAP estimation as it could give us the wrong result about the final learned parameters. There is a high chance that a different dataset could give us entirely different learned parameters that are far apart in the parameter space from the ones learned from the original dataset. This is what Bayesian learning tries to solve. It models the uncertainty in the parameter space explicitly.

Consider an example of the distribution of parameters given a dataset of left-handed and right-handed people. The distribution is shown in the following diagram:

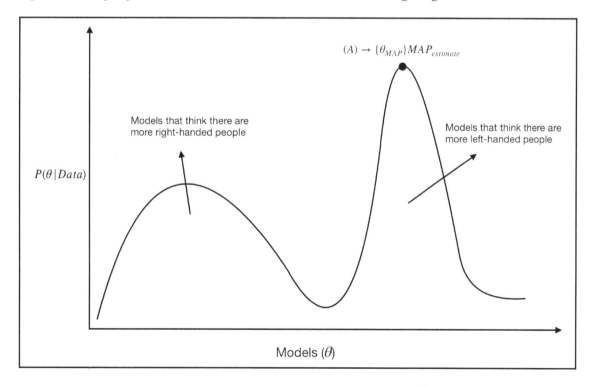

A MAP estimation that maximizes the probability of parameters (θ) from the data would converge to point A. However, most of the probability mass lies in the region where models favor *more right-handed people* and it aligns with the ground truth that there are more right-handed people in the world than there are left-handed.

So, in Bayesian learning, the focus is to solve posterior over parameters, $P(\theta|Data)$, to model this uncertainty in the parameters explicitly.

Understanding directed graphical models

We will now study directed graphical models briefly before we delve into probabilistic models for one-shot learning. A directed graphical model (also known as a Bayesian network) is defined with random variables connected with directed edges, as in the parent-child relationship. One such Bayesian network is shown in the following diagram:

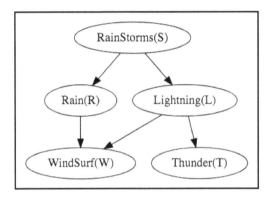

The joint distribution over random variables in this graph **S**, **R**, **L**, **W**, and **T** can be broken into multiple distributions by a simple chain rule:

$$P(S,R,L,W,T) = P(S)P(R|S)P(L|R,S)P(W|L,R,S)P(T|W,L,R,S)$$

The conditional distributions on the right side of the preceding equation have a large number of parameters. This is because each distribution is conditioned on many variables and each conditioned variable has its own outcome space. This effect is even more prominent if we go further down in the graph when we have a huge set of conditioned variables. Consequently, to learn this huge set of parameters for each conditional distribution, we need a large amount of labeled data, which is usually not available in modern machine learning tasks.

This is where the directed graphical model comes into the picture. It asserts some conditional independencies in the probability which simplifies the equation described previously. Each variable in a directed graphical model is conditionally independent of its non-descendants given its parents. A directed graphical model is nothing but a representation of conditional independencies. More formally, if X_i is a vertex in the directed graph, V is the number of vertices, and $X_{pa(t)}$ are all of the parents of vertex X_t, then the joint probability distribution over all vertices could be written as follows:

$$P(X_{1:v}) = \prod_{t=1}^{V} P(X_t | X_{pa(t)})$$

Given this, the joint distribution defined in the preceding equation simplifies to the following:

$$P(S,R,L,W,T) = P(S)P(R|S,)P(L|S)P(W|R,L)P(T|W,L)$$

This reduces the number of the parameters in the model and makes it easy to learn the model with comparatively less data.

Overview of probabilistic methods

Humans' conceptual learning tends to differ from machine learning in two major aspects. Consider an example of handwritten digits from a large vocabulary in the following diagram:

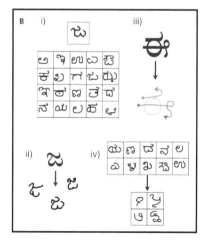

Firstly, people tend to learn meaningful information about objects, for example, object boundaries, from just one or a few examples and classify them with high accuracy (refer to the **i)** part in the preceding diagram). On the other hand, deep learning models need lots of labeled data to achieve human-level performance on tasks such as object recognition.

Secondly, humans learn a vast majority of functions from just one example, for example, creating new characters (refer to the **ii)** part in the preceding diagram), decomposing objects/characters into various parts and relations (refer to the **iii)** part in the preceding diagram), and developing new, meaningful concepts/characters (refer to the **iv)** part in the preceding diagram) from existing knowledge about existing concepts. On the contrary, deep learning models either require special loss functions and architectures for each task, which is usually not practical owing to very limited labeled data available for the task.

How do people tend to learn such rich, robust representations of the objects and concepts from just one example?

The learning theory states that more data (not less) is required to learn more complicated models that generalize well. But humans tend to learn far richer representations that generalize extremely well from highly sparse data.

Probabilistic models aim to bridge the gap between data-hungry machine models and highly robust *learning-to-learn* methodology adopted by humans. In this chapter, we will discuss two lines of probabilistic approaches that have gained wide success in learning various tasks from very little data:

- The first approach explicitly models object parts, subparts, and relations between them to learn a concept (object). This can be used to classify new objects from one, or only a few, examples and draw new types of objects from a predefined list of parts and subparts.
- The second approach, based on deep learning methods, does a one-shot classification task by learning new classes from an initial, large set of training data with only one image from these classes, and lots of images from other classes. This approach defines latent variables as priors on concepts (classes). The initial large set of training data helps in learning strong priors about concepts that are used thereafter to classify new objects from one-shot classes.

Bayesian program learning

Bayesian Program Learning (BPL) proceeds in three steps:

1. In the first step, which is a generative model, BPL learns new concepts by building them compositionally from parts (refer to **iii)** of the A side in the diagram of the *Model* section), subparts (refer to **ii)** of the A side in the following diagram), and their spatial relations (refer to **iv)** of the A side in the following diagram). For example, it can sample new types of concepts (or, in this case, handwritten characters) from parts and subparts and combine them in new ways.
2. In the second step, the concepts sampled in the first step form another lower-level generative model to produce new examples as shown in the **v)** part of the A side.
3. The final step renders raw character level images. Hence, BPL is a generative model for generative models. The pseudocode for this generative model is shown on the B side of the following diagram.

Model

Given our directed graphical model as shown in the A side, the joint distribution on types, ψ; a set of M tokens, $\theta^{(1)}, \ldots, \theta^{(M)}$; and their corresponding raw images, $I^{(1)}, \ldots, I^{(M)}$, factorizes as follows:

$$P(\psi, \theta^{(1)}, \ldots, \theta^{(M)}, I^{(1)}, \ldots, I^{(M)})$$
$$= P(\psi) \prod_{m=1}^{M} P(I^{(m)} | \theta^{(m)}) P(\theta^{(m)} | \psi)$$

The three generative processes are type generation ($P(\psi)$), token generation $P(\theta^{(m)}|\psi^{(m)})$ (), and image generation ($P(I^{(m)}|\theta^{(m)})$), and are discussed with their pseudocode in the following diagram:

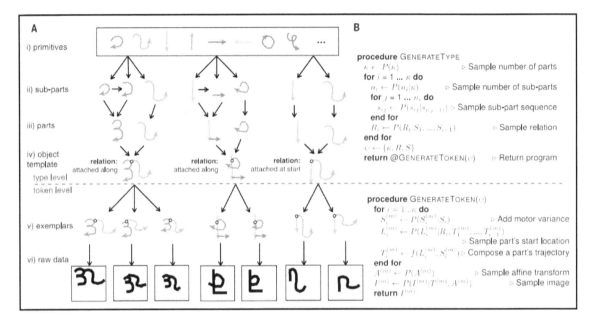

Type generation

Handwritten character types (ψ) are abstract schema between parts and subparts of the character and the relations among them. Reflecting the process of writing a character in real life, character parts, S_i, form one stroke of a pen-down to pen-lift operation. These character strokes are formed by subparts, $s_{i1}, \cdots s_{in_i}$, denoting brief pauses of the pen. The pseudocode to generate a new character type is shown in the B side of the preceding diagram and proceeds as follows:

1. To generate a new character type, the model first samples the number of parts (k) and the number of subparts (n_i) for each part. The sampling parameters come from their empirical distribution in the training dataset. The training data also provides a predefined set of primitives of the subparts.

2. Each character part is produced by sampling subparts from the predefined set so that the probability of sampling the next subpart is conditioned on the previous one.

3. A relation, R_i, is sampled for the part, S_i, which defines how this part is joined with the previous parts.

Token generation

Character tokens, $\theta^{(m)}$, are produced from parts and relations by modeling how ink flows from pen to paper. The pseudocode for token generation is described on the B side of the preceding diagram. First, a noise (called motor variance here) is added to scale and control points of subparts to define stroke (or part) trajectory, $S^{(m)}$. The trajectory's precise start location, $L^{(m)}$, is decided from relation, R_i. Finally, transformations, $A^{(m)}$, are applied to ease out probabilistic inference.

Image generation

The raw binary character image, $I^{(m)}$, is generated with a stochastic rendering function, which maps the stroke trajectory with grayscale ink. This is achieved by assigning independent Bernoulli probabilities to each pixel.

BPL is a highly intuitive model that can model concepts with simple programs under the Bayesian framework. The parameters of the probability distributions are learned from the training data. On single-shot computer vision tasks of classification and generation, the model's performance is at par with human-level performance, with data requirements much less than some recent deep learning models. The probabilistic programs studied here are quite basic and suited for fairly easy character recognition tasks. The BPL framework supports the design of more complex programs that can model complex representations of various objects. For example, objects, such as vehicles, food items, animals, and even human faces, that have a clear and intuitive description in terms of parts and relations can be modeled with this framework. To this end, the BPL framework even supports modeling abstract knowledge such as natural language semantics and physical theories. Nevertheless, these probabilistic programs require manual labeling of data and its parts, subparts, and relations, which is a time-consuming process, whereas deep learning approaches learn these human-intuitive features as well deep abstract features on their own.

Discriminative k-shot learning

A very common approach for k-shot learning is to train a large model with a related task for which we have a large dataset. This model is then fine-tuned with the k-shot specific task. Hence, the knowledge from the large dataset is *distilled* into the model, which augments the learning of new related tasks from just a few examples. In 2003, Bakker and Heskes introduced a probabilistic model for k-shot learning where all of the tasks share a common feature extractor but have a respective linear classifier with just a few task-specific parameters.

The probabilistic method to k-shot learning discussed here is very similar to the one introduced by Bakker and Heskes. This method solves the classification task (for images) by learning a probabilistic model from very little data. The idea is to use a powerful neural network that learns robust features from a large set of supervised data and combine it with the probabilistic model. The weights of the final layer of the neural network act as data that regularizes the weights of k-shot sub-model in a Bayesian manner.

The learning framework comprises four phases:

- Representation learning
- Concept learning
- K-shot learning
- K-shot testing

The framework with its four phases is shown in the following diagram. They are discussed more formally in the following subsections:

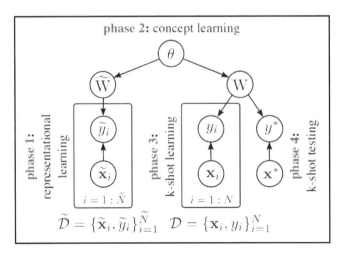

Representational learning

In the first phase (representation learning), the CNN (Φ_φ) is trained with a large dataset, $\widetilde{D}$, that trains the parameters, φ and $\widetilde{W}$, of the network. After this, these parameters, φ, are fixed and shared across later phases. The activations from the last layer of the CNN are mapped to two sets of softmax layers, parametrized by $\widetilde{W}$ and W. Parameters $\widetilde{W}$ correspond to $\widetilde{C}$ classes in the large dataset, $\widetilde{D}$, and parameters W correspond to C classes in the k-shot task's dataset, D. This is shown in the following diagram:

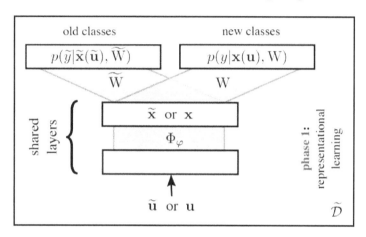

Probabilistic model of the weights

It is assumed that there is very little uncertainty in softmax weights, $\widetilde{W}$, learned in phase 1 due to the large dataset, $\widetilde{D}$. Combining this approximation with the structure of the graphical model in the preceding diagram, we can get rid of the original dataset, $\widetilde{D}$, and use the MAP estimate of $\widetilde{W}$ (W^{MAP}) in the concept learning and k-shot learning phase. A complete probabilistic model follows these steps:

1. The k-shot learning process combines information in two datasets, $\widetilde{D}$ and D, to generate the posterior distribution on W as follows:

$$P(W|D,\widetilde{D}) \propto P(W,D,\widetilde{D}) = P(\widetilde{D})P(W|\widetilde{D})P(D|\widetilde{D},W) \qquad (1)$$

2. From the graphical model, in the preceding diagram, we know that D is conditionally independent of $\widetilde{D}$ given the parent W, so that we have the following:

$$P(D|W, \widetilde{D}) = P(D|W) = \prod_n p(y_n|x_n, W)$$

Equation 1 hence becomes the following:

$$P(W|D, \widetilde{D}) \propto P(\widetilde{D})P(W|\widetilde{D}) \prod_n P(y_n|x_n, W)$$

3. We can absorb the term $P(\widetilde{D})$ into the constant of proportionality so that the preceding equation becomes the following:

$$P(W|D, \widetilde{D}) \propto P(W|\widetilde{D}) \prod_n P(y_n|x_n, W) \qquad (2)$$

$$\text{where } P(W|\widetilde{D}) = \int_\theta P(W|\theta)P(\theta|\widetilde{D})d\theta$$

The main challenge is to compute the posterior over hyperparameters θ given the initial dataset, $\widetilde{D}$, which causes inference in this model to be intractable. Since a large initial dataset is used to learn the weights, $\widetilde{W}$, the posterior distribution, $P(\widetilde{W}|\widetilde{D})$, can be safely approximated with its MAP estimate, that is, $P(\widetilde{W}|\widetilde{D}) \approx \delta(W - W^{MAP})$. Hence, we can get rid of $\widetilde{D}$ in equation 2 and replace it with $\widetilde{W}$.

Choosing a model for the weights

Given the graphical model, we can write the joint distribution over the concept hyperparameters (θ) and model weights (W, $\widetilde{W}$) as follows:

$$P(\theta, W, \widetilde{W}) = P(\theta)P(W|\theta)P(\widetilde{W}|\theta) \qquad (3)$$

Two simple but reasonable assumptions are made to make the machinery computationally tractable:

- First, the hidden weights, W and $\widetilde{W}$, from the last hidden layer to softmax are treated as independent for each class.

- Second, the distribution of weights, W and $\widetilde{W}$, given θ, $P(\widetilde{w}_{c'}|\theta)$, and $P(w_c|\theta)$ is identical.

The joint distribution in equation 3 then reduces to the following:

$$P(\theta, \widetilde{W}, W,) = P(\theta) \prod_{c'=1}^{\widetilde{C}} P(\widetilde{w}_{c'}|\theta) \prod_{c=1}^{C} P(w_c|\theta)$$

A simple Gaussian model is used for weights $P(w|\theta) = \mathcal{N}(w|\mu, \sum)$ with its conjugate Normal-inverse-Wishart prior, $P(\theta) = P(\mu, \sum) = \mathcal{NIW}(\mu_0, \kappa_0, \Lambda_0, v_0)$, and estimates MAP solutions for parameters, $\theta^{MAP} = \{\mu^{MAP}, \overset{MAP}{\sum}\}$.

This leads to distributions being simplified to the following:

$$P(W|\widetilde{D}) \approx P(W|\widetilde{W}^{MAP}) = \mathcal{N}(W|\mu^{MAP}, \overset{MAP}{\sum}) \qquad (4)$$

The posterior distribution of new weights W during k-shot learning (equation 2) reduces to the following expression:

$$P(W|D, \widetilde{D}) \propto \mathcal{N}(W|\mu^{MAP}, \overset{MAP}{\sum}) \prod_{n=1}^{N} p(y_n|x_n, W)$$

Computation and approximation for each phase

Following the discussion on the machinery of the preceding model, the following subsections summarize all of the computations and approximations in the four phases of the discriminative k-shot model.

Phase 1 – representation learning

Initially, deep learning trains the feature extractor CNN, Φ_φ. The activations of the last layer for the input image (u), $x = \Phi_\varphi(u)$, are used in the following phases. The softmax weights for the classes in the original dataset are the MAP estimates $\widetilde{W}^{MAP}$.

Phase 2 – concept learning

A probabilistic model is fit directly to the MAP weights, $P(\theta|\widetilde{W}) \propto P(\theta)P(\widetilde{W}|\theta)$. For conjugate models, the posterior distribution is obtained analytically; otherwise, the MAP estimate of $P(\theta|\widetilde{W})$ is used.

Phase 3 – k-shot learning

The posterior over the softmax weights W, $P(W|D,\widetilde{W}^{MAP}) \propto P(W|\widetilde{W}^{MAP})\prod_{n=1}^{N} P(y_n|x_n, W)$, is intractable. It is approximated by either using MAP estimate W^{MAP} or through sampling $W_m \propto P(W|D,\widetilde{W}^{MAP})$. It must be noted that $P(W|\widetilde{W}^{MAP}) = \int P(W|\theta)P(\theta|\widetilde{W}^{MAP})d\theta$ is analytic for conjugate models. However, if θ is estimated from MAP estimation in phase 2, then $P(W|\widetilde{W}^{MAP}) \approx P(W|\theta^{MAP})$ is used as explained in equation 4.

Phase 4 – k-shot testing

The inference at k-shot testing time $P(y^*|x^*, D, \widetilde{W}^{MAP}) = \int p(y^*|x^*, W)P(W|D, \widetilde{W}^{MAP})dW$ is intractable, so approximations are used here. If the MAP estimate for W (W^{MAP}) is used from phase 3, then $P(y^*|x^*, D, \widetilde{W}^{MAP}) = P(y^*|x^*, W^{MAP})$. If samples are retuned in phase 3, then, $P(y^*|x^*, D, \widetilde{W}^{MAP}) = \frac{1}{M}\sum_{m=1}^{M} p(y^*|x^*, W_m)$ is used.

On the miniImageNet dataset (composed of 100 classes with 600 images from each class), this method achieves state-of-the-art results on one-shot and five-shot learning by a wide margin. It's a step closer to unifying the fields of probabilistic models and deep learning, which, when combined, develops really powerful models leveraging strong mathematical guarantees from probabilistic fields and powerful robust features from deep learning models. Discriminative k-shot learning methods still require large amounts of labeled training data to train the deep learning-based feature extractor. On the other hand, the Bayesian program learning method makes use of inductive biases in the model and hand-engineered features and hence needs less labeled training data.

Summary

In this chapter, we learned about developing probabilistic models within a Bayesian framework that vastly reduces data requirements and achieves human-level performance. From the example of the handwritten characters discussed previously, we also observed how probabilistic models can not only learn how to classify characters but learn the underlying concept, that is, apply the acquired knowledge in new ways, such as generating similar characters and generating entirely new characters from only a few characters in a set, as well as parsing a character into parts and relations.

However, human learners approach new learning tasks armed with extensive prior experience gained from many experiences with rich overlapping structures. To mimic human learning, the graphical structure needs to have more dependencies and rich inductive biases need to be built into the models. It is also noted that humans have a good sense of the physics of an object (its shape, movement, and other mechanics) at a very young age. The intuitive physics of the objects is not captured implicitly by learning models, and neither is it embedded explicitly in them. The integration of intuitive physics (similar to the physics embedded in game engines), with probabilistic models and deep learning, is an important step toward more robust few-shot learning. Finally, owing to prior knowledge being embedded in probabilistic models in the form of strong priors and a graphical structure, they are less data-hungry when compared with deep learning models that have to learn the task from scratch. But this comes at the cost of computational challenges for efficient inference in probabilistic models. At inference time, these models have to search a vast probabilistic space, which is not practical with modern computers. In contrast, the deep learning models have exact and computationally inexpensive inference. Recent work tackles this inference challenge in graphical models by *amortizing* probabilistic inference computations with feed-forward mappings that could be learned with paired generative/recognition networks. This presents another promising line of research that brings deep learning and probabilistic models closer.

Further reading

To learn more about the topics covered in this chapter, read the following papers:

- *Human-level concept learning through probabilistic program induction*: `https://web.mit.edu/cocosci/Papers/Science-2015-Lake-1332-8.pdf`
- *A Bayesian approach to unsupervised one-shot learning of object categories*: `http://vision.stanford.edu/documents/Fei-Fei_ICCV03.pdf`
- *Discriminative k-shot learning using probabilistic models*: `https://arxiv.org/pdf/1706.00326.pdf`
- *Building machines that learn and think like people*: `http://web.stanford.edu/class/psych209/Readings/LakeEtAlBBS.pdf`
- *One-shot learning of simple visual concepts*: `https://cims.nyu.edu/~brenden/LakeEtAl2011CogSci.pdf`
- *One-shot learning with a hierarchical nonparametric Bayesian model*: `https://www.cs.cmu.edu/~rsalakhu/papers/MIT-CSAIL-TR-2010-052.pdf`

6
Conclusions and Other Approaches

In this book, we have learned about various forms of architectures for deep learning, and various techniques and methods, ranging from manual feature extraction to the variational Bayesian framework. One-shot learning is a particularly active field of research as it focuses on building a type of machine consciousness more closely based on human neural abilities. With advancements made in the deep learning community over the past 5 years, we can at least say that we are on the path to developing a machine that can learn multiple tasks at once, just as a human can. In this chapter, we will see what other alternatives there are to one-shot learning, and discuss other approaches that haven't been explored in depth in this book.

The following topics will be covered:

- Recent advancements
- Related fields
- Applications

Recent advancements

In the deep learning community, there are various other approaches that have been proposed for one-shot learning, such as generative modeling using GANs, image deformation meta-networks, representative based metric learning, and so on. So far, we have seen models doing classification using one-shot learning, but there are advancements currently being made in object detection and semantic segmentation as well. In this section, we will touch upon some of the recent papers from major machine learning-based conferences (for example, CVPR, NeurIPS, ICLR, and so on).

Metric-based learning is one of the older methods to approach one-shot learning. Though this area is old, there are plenty of aspects of it that are still being explored. The research work on the topic *Revisiting local descriptor based image-to-class measure for few-shot learning* (`https://arxiv.org/abs/1903.12290`) is a good example of this. In this paper, the authors proposed a convolutional neural network architecture called **D4N** (**deep nearest neighbor neural network**), which extracts image-level features. Its key difference to other neural network architectures is the replacement of the final layer with a local descriptor-based image-to-class measure.

Finding task-relevant features for few-shot learning by category traversal (`https://arxiv.org/abs/1905.11116`) has also made good contributions in improving metric learning methods by introducing a plugin framework. In this paper, the authors talk about how well-known metric learning methods such as Siamese networks and matching networks focus on one task at a time, instead of learning about all tasks as a whole. The **category traversal module** (**CTM**) plugin component learns important dimension features by going through all support tasks. CTM extracts the common feature embeddings for similar categories and unique across different categories with the help of a concentrator and projector unit. Using the output of CTM, we can potentially add a strong prior to our meta-learner, which can give us faster and better optimization. By using this framework, they showed a significant improvement in the metric-based learning method.

There have also been some notable contributions in the domains of object detection and semantic segmentation. Let's discuss two of those approaches.

Object detection in few-shot domains

RepMet: Representative-based metric learning for classification and few-shot object detection (`https://arxiv.org/abs/1806.04728`) is a few-shot learning object detection method. In this paper, the authors proposed a variant of a feature pyramid network for region proposals of objects, and on top of it, they added a metric-based classifier that classifies proposed regions on the basis of distance from learned class representatives. They also made a contribution to the research community by setting up a benchmark on the ImageNet dataset for the few-shot object detection task.

Similarly, *One-shot object detection with co-attention and co-excitation* (`https://arxiv.org/abs/1911.12529`) also works on filtering on the basis of proposed regions using traditional vision methods. In this work, the authors assumed that a target image will be provided along with a query image. For example, if we are looking to detect a pen holder, the target image will be a pen holder, whereas a query image will be a pen holder on a table. In this approach, we first extract spatial information about an object from the target image followed by contextual objects from the query image. Contextual and spatial information plays an important role in determining objects. For example, if there is a table depicted, the likelihood of a pen holder being present increases. This is similar to how humans learn using context. This model also takes the help of context by passing input into the attention model.

Image segmentation in few-shot domains

The research work *CANet: Class-agnostic segmentation networks with iterative refinement and attentive few-shot learning* (`https://arxiv.org/abs/1903.02351`) is proof of potential growth in the medical imaging industry. In this paper, the authors proposed a two-level framework for semantic segmentation: a **dense comparison module** (**DCM**) and an **iterative optimization module** (**IOM**). DCM does dense feature comparison among training-set examples and test-set examples by extracting features using common ResNet architecture, whereas IOM refines results over iteration through a residual block+CNN and an **atrous spatial pyramid pooling** (**ASPP**) module.

Similarly, *PANet: Few-shot image semantic segmentation with prototype alignment* (`https://arxiv.org/abs/1908.06391`) tackles the few-shot segmentation problem through the perspective of the metric learning approach. This paper also proposed an alignment network to better utilize the information extracted from the support set. In PANet, initially, the network learns class-specific representations from a few support images within a specific embedding space and later performs segmentation on query/target images by matching each pixel to the learned class-specific representations. Using this approach, PANet uses important insight from the support set and provides more solid generalization in few-shot segmentation scenarios.

As we can see, these solutions are for cases when we have limited data. How do we quantify what is limited and what is enough? We need to look at the capacity of the model architecture that we wish to train, and the complexity of the problem we wish to solve. Similar to one-shot learning, there are other approaches that have been proposed by researchers over the years that also aim to solve the problem of limited data. In the next section, we will learn about such domains of machine learning, and how efficient they are in comparison to one-shot learning.

Related fields

As we know, one-shot learning is a sub-field of ML. There are different relevant solutions that are very similar to the one-shot learning approach, yet slightly different in their solution approach. Such problems can be solved by using one-shot learning algorithms as well. Let's go through each of the relevant fields of ML and observe how similar they are to the one-shot learning problem:

- Semi-supervised learning
- Imbalanced learning
- Meta-learning
- Transfer learning

Semi-supervised learning

Suppose we have 10,000 data points where only 20,000 are labeled and 80,000 are unlabeled. In such cases, we would employ semi-supervised learning. In semi-supervised learning, we use unlabeled data to gain more of an understanding of the population structure in general. Semi-supervised learning goes through a pseudo-labeling technique to increase the training set; that is, we train a model using 20,000 labeled datasets and use it on equally sized test data points to create pseudo-labels for them. The following diagram illustrates a semi-supervised learning architecture:

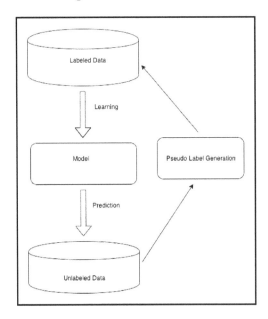

After obtaining pseudo-labels, we concatenate real labels with pseudo-labels and real features with pseudo-features. After concatenation, we train a new model, which is proven to be more accurate than the initial model. We keep doing this until optimal accuracy is achieved.

Imbalanced learning

In the imbalanced learning scenario, we have an imbalanced dataset; that is, we have more samples from one class than we do from other categories. This is also popularly known as a **skewed distribution dataset.** Let's take a look at some popular methods for dealing with a skewed dataset:

- **Choice of metric**: There are various forms of metrics that can help in assessing the accuracy of a model, such as a confusion matrix, precision, recall, and F1-score.
- **Choice of algorithm**: Parametric algorithms learn their parameters through the dataset, so if the dataset is biased, it is most likely that the parametric model will also be biased. Non-parametric approaches (for example, k-Nearest Neighbor) and ensembles (for example, AdaBoost, XGBoost, and so on) are proven to be the best approaches when it comes to a biased dataset.
- **Choice of data sampling methods**: Data sampling can also be considered to ensure that the dataset doesn't remain skewed.

This approach is close to one-shot learning, as the machine learning model we are expected to create should be able to learn distribution from a few examples.

 To learn more about different forms of metrics, please refer to `Chapter 2`, *Metrics-Based Methods*.

Meta-learning

Meta-learning has recently generated a lot of attention in the research community. Most of the methods that have been discussed in this book are meta-learning type methods, such as model agnostic meta-learning and meta networks. Meta-learning is an approach to train a model on different tasks and then use commonly learned features for a specific task. It helps the model to learn a strong prior across many tasks, which helps a model to reach optimization with limited data. In simpler words, meta-learning is an approach to train a model to *learn to learn* any objective.

Transfer learning

Transfer learning refers to the technique of using knowledge gleaned from solving one problem and using that to solve a different problem. The following is an illustration of a simplistic view of the transfer learning approach:

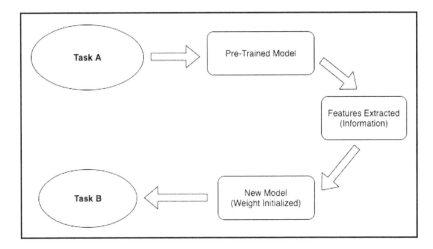

In other words, a neural network model trained on one dataset can be used for other datasets by fine-tuning the former network, just like how we can use Siamese networks trained on different domain datasets (such as the MNIST dataset) to extract better features for signature matching, handwriting matching, and so on. Transfer learning has attracted a lot of attention in the field of deep learning and has been proven to be very useful for a number of applications; however, we are unable to use it in non-common domains, such as manufacturing, medicine, chemicals, and so on, due to data limitations.

Applications

Theoretically, there are various applications for one-shot learning, but only recently has it started being used in real-world scenarios. Recent advancements have been made using one-shot learning, such as writing SQL codes, improving deformed medical images, and running signature verification. There are several other domains that are still under research. Companies such as OpenAI, Google, Microsoft, and Amazon are investing heavily in AI research. Solving one-shot learning would mean creating a mechanical brain with the abilities of a human. This advancement could save lives in a number of ways: it could pave the way for rare-disease detection, solve the global food crisis, or optimize supply-chain models.

In this book, we have explored a few of the possible approaches to one-shot learning. If you wish to explore more, please refer to the *Further reading* section.

Further reading

To explore more about this chapter, refer to the following works:

- *Hands-On Meta-Learning*: https://www.packtpub.com/big-data-and-business-intelligence/hands-meta-learning-python
- *Revisiting local descriptor based image-to-class measure for few-shot learning*: https://arxiv.org/pdf/1903.12290.pdf
- *Finding task-relevant features for few-shot learning by category traversal*: https://arxiv.org/pdf/1905.11116.pdf
- *RepMet: Representative-based metric learning for classification and few-shot object detection*: https://arxiv.org/abs/1806.04728
- *One-shot object detection with co-attention and co-excitation*: https://arxiv.org/pdf/1911.12529.pdf
- *CANet: Class-agnostic segmentation networks with iterative refinement and attentive few-shot learning*: https://arxiv.org/pdf/1903.02351.pdf
- *PANet: Few-shot image semantic segmentation with prototype alignment*: https://arxiv.org/pdf/1908.06391.pdf

Other Books You May Enjoy

If you enjoyed this book, you may be interested in these other books by Packt:

Hands-On Meta Learning with Python
Sudharsan Ravichandiran

ISBN: 978-1-78953-420-7

- Understand the basics of meta learning methods, algorithms, and types
- Build voice and face recognition models using a siamese network
- Learn the prototypical network along with its variants
- Build relation networks and matching networks from scratch
- Implement MAML and Reptile algorithms from scratch in Python
- Work through imitation learning and adversarial meta learning
- Explore task agnostic meta learning and deep meta learning

Advanced Deep Learning with Python
Ivan Vasilev

ISBN: 978-1-78995-617-7

- Cover advanced and state-of-the-art neural network architectures
- Understand the theory and math behind neural networks
- Train DNNs and apply them to modern deep learning problems
- Use CNNs for object detection and image segmentation
- Implement generative adversarial networks (GANs) and variational autoencoders to generate new images
- Solve natural language processing (NLP) tasks, such as machine translation, using sequence-to-sequence models
- Understand DL techniques, such as meta-learning and graph neural networks

Leave a review - let other readers know what you think

Please share your thoughts on this book with others by leaving a review on the site that you bought it from. If you purchased the book from Amazon, please leave us an honest review on this book's Amazon page. This is vital so that other potential readers can see and use your unbiased opinion to make purchasing decisions, we can understand what our customers think about our products, and our authors can see your feedback on the title that they have worked with Packt to create. It will only take a few minutes of your time, but is valuable to other potential customers, our authors, and Packt. Thank you!

Index

overview 26
probabilistic methods
    overview 119, 120
probabilistic model
    of weights 125, 126
    selecting, for weights 126, 127

R

relevant fields, ML
    about 134
    imbalanced learning 135
    meta-learning 135
    semi-supervised learning 134
    transfer learning 136
representation learning
    about 125
    computation and approximation 128
result analysis 14
root mean square 44

S

semi-supervised learning 134
Siamese networks implementations
    about 41

MNIST dataset 42, 44, 45, 47, 48
Siamese networks
    about 29, 30
    applications 34
    architecture 30, 31
    contrastive loss function 32, 33
    preprocessing 31, 32
    triplet loss function 33, 34
skewed dataset, methods
    choice of algorithm 135
    choice of data sampling methods 135
    choice of metric 135
skewed distribution dataset 135

T

token generation 123
triplet loss function 33, 34

V

virtual environment
    setting up 16

W

weight vector 65

www.ingramcontent.com/pod-product-compliance
Lightning Source LLC
Chambersburg PA
CBHW080534060326
40690CB00022B/5131